THE PREDICAMENT
of the
CHURCH

THE PREDICAMENT OF THE CHURCH

Contemporary Essays

by

A. D. LINDSAY

A. M. MURRAY

BENEDICTA ROWE

F. B. WELBOURN

EMIL BRUNNER

M. VERSFELD

PATRICIA OWEN

TIRAN NERSOYAN

C. G. SCHWEITZER

LUTTERWORTH PRESS

LONDON and REDHILL

*Printed in Great Britain by
The Camelot Press Limited, London and Southampton*

CONTENTS

NOTE

D URING the year 1943 a number of articles appeared at points so far removed from each other as New York, London, Madras and Cape Town. Men and women in different lands were trying to bring Christian thought to bear upon contemporary problems. Certain of these essays appear here together as a group under a title belonging primarily to one of them, but only in the case of two is production here closely identical with the original form. In the case of the others, the authors have either availed themselves of opportunity to expand, emend or contract, or have allowed editorial request and suggestion to bring about some re-shaping of the material. In one case the material is wholly new.

Grateful acknowledgment is made to the Editors of *Religion in Life* (New York), *The Christian News-Letter* and *The International Review of Missions* (London), and the Christian Council of South Africa, for permission to use material; as also to the National Christian Council of India, Burma and Ceylon.

Duty to God and State

by
A. D. LINDSAY
Master of Balliol

I

GOD AND MY NEIGHBOUR

THE great gift which the inspiration of the Hebrew prophets gave to mankind was a vision of God—the only worthy object of boundless reverence and absolute devotion—as containing two infinities, the infinity of the universe and infinity of goodness. Such is the theme, for example, of Psalm xix: "The heavens declare the glory of God; and the firmament sheweth his handywork"; and then, at verse 7: "The law of the Lord is perfect, converting the soul: the testimony of the Lord is sure, making wise the simple." It is easy for us, thanks to modern science, to believe in the infinity of the universe; but it is not so easy to believe in the infinity of goodness. For the eternal principles of right and wrong, when they find realization among human beings, reflect historical and imperfect conditions. It seems absurd to many people that the infinite universe which modern science reveals should have anything to do with something so local and variable and accidental as morality appears to be. For when we consider the forms in which goodness becomes realized among men—moralities and customs, laws and moral codes and institutions—they all reflect passing conditions in an historical process; they are various and discrepant; there seems to be nothing infinite about them. Men even pursue this line of thought so far as to deny that goodness has any reality of its own: it is what pays a particular society or a particular class or even a particular individual to do at a particular moment. If that were so, to talk of the goodness of God would be an absurdity, and Christianity would be an absurdity.

This reluctance to believe that goodness has anything to do

7

with infinity comes partly from sheer misunderstanding. Men often look now at moral phenomena as superficially as in the past they looked at physical phenomena, and their moral views are as crude as past views of the physical world have been. They see the historical nature of morals. They forget that all progress in morality, all bettering of laws, all improvement in institutions, has been brought about by men and women who regarded goodness as having an absolute claim upon them: who were not prepared to sit down with things as they found them: who would not acquiesce in things because they were customary or approved by society or institutions: who were impelled by something to go beyond the given and the customary and the orthodox, beyond the fashion of this age or that. They were such as the heroes of faith described in the eleventh chapter of the Hebrews, who "confessed that they were strangers and pilgrims on the earth. . . . And truly if they had been mindful of that country from whence they came out, they might have had opportunity to have returned. But now they desire a better country, that is, an heavenly: wherefore God is not ashamed to be called their God; for He hath prepared for them a city."

Moral codes and customs and institutions are historical and imperfect realizations of absolute principles; but they are both these things—imperfect and historical and embodiments of something neither imperfect nor historical. So are physical phenomena, which we could never understand apart from the realization of a principle at work in a process.

But our failure to believe actively in the goodness of God or, if you like, the infinity of goodness, does not come only from intellectual misunderstanding. It comes from our own recurring moral failure—our readiness to live on the moral capital others have accumulated. "Your fathers slew the prophets and ye build their tombs," said Jesus to the Pharisees. We all of us do that: reverence the prophets when they are safely dead and can be entombed, on the strict understanding that that absolves us from having anything to do with living prophets. We are all inclined to let the moral demands of our set or station, or our duties to our kindred or our own society, serve as our absolute, thus denying God's infinity.

8

When we do that, we are in practice asserting that goodness is a local and accidental business: what happens to serve or suit ourselves, our friends, our class, or our country; and when we do that, we are, however pious we may be about it, blaspheming against God.

If we believe in God, we cannot regard as absolute our duties to anything less than God: we must be prepared to subordinate all claims from limited things—kindred, class, family, society, state—to the claims of infinite goodness: when we refuse to listen to the demand that we should go out beyond the closed circle of our customary morality, we are denying God.

The demands of infinite goodness are absolute though not infinite; the particular demands of this or that society are secondary. Jesus gave His approval to the form in which the Old Testament had summed up this teaching. In Mark xii. 28 we read:

> "And one of the scribes came and, having heard them reasoning together, and perceiving that he had answered them well, asked him, Which is the first commandment of all? And Jesus answered him, The first of all the commandments is, Hear, O Israel; The Lord our God is one Lord, and thou shalt love the Lord thy God with all thy heart, and with all thy soul, and with all thy mind, and with all thy strength: this is the first commandment. And the second is like, namely this, Thou shalt love thy neighbour as thyself. There is none other commandment greater than these."

"The second is like," Jesus said. That brings these two commandments into the close and vital relation which makes Christianity. Without that relation the first command will be unmeaning and the second conventional: we shall think the first is a command to piety in general, the second a command to do the social duties expected of us. But the New Testament teaching is that, while the commandment to love our neighbours follows the command to love God, if we do not love our neighbours we show that we do not love God. "He that loveth not his brother whom he hath seen, how can he love God whom he hath not seen?" Nor do we love

9

God if our love of our neighbours remains a conventional fulfilling of conventional duties: if our love of God does not put a certain absolute and universal quality into our social action.

Consider the parable of the good Samaritan. The story, in St. Luke's Gospel, Chapter x, starts with the same Old Testament reference:

> "And behold, a certain lawyer stood up, and tempted him, saying, Master, what shall I do to inherit eternal life? He said unto him, What is written in the law? how readest thou? And he answering said, Thou shalt love the Lord thy God with all thy heart, and with all thy soul, and with all thy strength, and with all thy mind; and thy neighbour as thyself. And he said unto him, Thou hast answered right: this do, and thou shalt live. But he, willing to justify himself, said unto Jesus, And who is my neighbour?"

And then Jesus tells the parable of the good Samaritan: of the man who was left half dead by the roadside; who was neglected by the priest and the Levite, though these had obligations and duties of their station to help him, and was helped by a Samaritan, a despised and hated outsider—like a Nazi being neglected by an S.S. man and helped by a Jew. And the parable ends, you remember, with the question:

> "Which now of these three, thinkest thou, was neighbour unto him that fell among thieves? And he said, He that shewed mercy on him. Then said Jesus unto him, Go, and do thou likewise."

The moral of the good Samaritan is that our special duties to other people should be determined by their need and our power to help. The man who fell among thieves was the Samaritan's neighbour because there he was, lying by the roadside, half dead, and there was the Samaritan on the spot. It is a mistake to suppose that the parable teaches universal benevolence or that everybody is our neighbour. It teaches that love lives in loving action. If it means action and not a vague well-meaningness, we cannot in that sense love everybody. Action must be specific and definite and limited: a choice of doing this rather than that: helping A rather than B. There is no escape from that. Indeed, the more loving the action is, and the more thought and care and understanding it displays, the smaller the number of persons on whom it is directed. You can, with the aid of an addressograph, send a printed postcard to hundreds of people in the time in which you can write only one long, intimate, worth-while letter. If the good Samaritan had contented himself with handing out to all distressed persons he met by the roadside assistance tickets to be handed by the recipient to the Jerusalem-Jericho Distressed Travellers' Aid Society, he might have handed out quite a number in the course of his journey and it might have cost him money, but he would never have been the subject of Jesus' parable. Plato said that in his ideal city all the citizens should be friends. Aristotle, with his usual dry common sense, comments that it would be a very watery friendship.

Read those chapters in Dickens' "Bleak House" which contain his fierce and penetrating satire on that kind of sham universal benevolence which makes stunt flights across continents and neglects immediate duties—the picture of Mrs. Jellyby. She took the natives of Borrioboola Gha as her neighbours—in the sense of the proper objects of her benevolence—and entirely neglected her home and children. Her family suffered, and the natives got little if any good. Dickens thinks she was a foolish woman. The text we have quoted above from St. John might be supplemented by adding: "He that loveth not his brother whom he hath seen, how can he love his brother whom he hath not seen?"

We are, then, to continue to love, not everybody, but our neighbour, as ourselves; and our neighbour is to be interpreted by this principle: he is our neighbour who most needs the help which we are able to give; and the claims of particular groups upon us—of family, of neighbourhood, of city and nation—are to be assessed on that principle. If we have special duties to our family, it is because loving action is most effective when based on knowledge and understanding and opportunity. Our neighbours—those nearest to us, in place or in living together or in familiarity—are normally those whom we can best help. Those social institutions which make up so much of our lives are necessary instruments of goodness. If they did not exist, if there was not the framework of custom, convention, and law within which our normal life goes on, life would be a struggle with anarchy and chaos. Kindness and friendship and the best kinds of human intercourse are killed in anarchy and fostered in the security of a well-ordered society; and so ordinary social institutions, the family, the nation, the state—imperfect as they are—are necessary instruments of goodness, and have claims on our allegiance as such. But they are not ends in themselves: they are means to the good life, and to be cherished as such.

For these reasons it *is* true that charity begins at home—but it is a poor pining charity which ends there. If it is really charity, it must spill over those customary and accepted claims and be prepared to listen to the demands of greater need that come from regions beyond those spheres of customary duty.

So far, I have hardly mentioned the State. I have been talking mainly of the conflicting claims of our smaller social groups with the wider claims, the kind of conflict which easily arises, for example, when a woman has to balance the call of missionary work against the claims of her family; or when a man feels called to leave his ordinary job and duties and volunteer to meet a call of special need. There is no rule to decide when we should so give up our obvious duties for a wider but less obvious call. The only rule is that we should be prepared to listen and respond to such calls when they come. There is, you remember, an inexorable saying of Jesus: "If any man come to me and hate not his father and mother and wife and children and brethren and sisters, yea and his own life also, he cannot be my disciple." We are to be prepared to give up all the natural and obvious calls upon us when God calls us: but He does not always or, indeed, often so call us. Most of us, most of the time, are called to serve God in the ordinary service of our ordinary duties, so long as we are ready for the wider call.

But the demands of the State seem somehow different from either the demands of a natural social group such as our family or our friends or our neighbours on the one hand, or the demands of outside need on the other. They are not so much demands as commands. They are fortified by sanctions, backed by force. They claim at all times, and especially at times like these, to cut across other obligations. They may demand everything of us up to our lives: they call on us to do things which many of us would not naturally do—to play our part in the State's use of force, not only to risk our lives but to fight and kill other men. How different is this compulsory relationship either from the quiet, ordinary, secure life which most of us usually live, or from the devoted life of the missionary or the real lover of men or of the saint! How can our duty to God square with our duty to this compulsory order?

"And they asked him, saying, Master, we know that thou sayest and teachest rightly, neither acceptest thou the person of any but teachest the way of God truly. Is it lawful for us to give tribute unto Cæsar, or no? And he said unto them, Render unto Cæsar the things which be Cæsar's, and unto God the things which be God's."

Yes, but what are Cæsar's things and what are God's? That is the question we must next consider.

II

CHURCH, STATE AND COMMUNITY

"Render unto Cæsar the things that be Cæsar's, and to God the things that be God's."

"Cæsar" was a symbol then, and may be a symbol now for us, of the compulsion of the State. How is that compulsion, with the commands it puts upon us to do things which we should not otherwise have done, to be reconciled with our duty to God?

Of course, our "Cæsar" nowadays is very different from the Cæsar the Jews knew. To the Jews Cæsar represented a conquering power, against which they had been continually in revolt; which imposed taxes upon them without consulting them and spent them largely for the benefit of Rome. Our Cæsar is our own government; we elect it; our representatives can criticise its doings. Over and above its compulsion, our Cæsar—that is, our State—does all manner of good and benevolent things of which we heartily approve, of whose beneficence we have no doubt. The most hated characters in the New Testament are the tribute-gatherers—the publicans as they are called. We should never dream of referring to our Civil Servants as proverbially hated characters, as the Gospels continually do.

But though the Jews' Cæsar was imposed upon them and ours is our own choice, the Jews' Cæsar performed one service which ours also performs. Rome kept order and maintained law. The Jews of the Gospel's time, and the early Christians of the first few centuries, lived in a world where peace was on the whole preserved, and law maintained, by the force of Rome. They lived within the framework of security which that force provided. It is in recognition of that fact that St. Paul, in the thirteenth chapter of the Epistle to the Romans, tells Christians to be "subject unto the higher powers." "Rulers are not a terror to good works, but to the evil. Wilt thou then not be afraid of the power? Do that which is good, and thou shalt have praise of the same. For he is the minister of God to thee for good. But if thou do that which is evil, be afraid; for he beareth not the sword in vain": and so on.

What St. Paul has to say is not the conclusion of the matter. The Apostle recognized that rulers might give orders which Christians had to disobey, as when Peter and the Apostles in the Acts were told not to teach in the name of Jesus, and answered: "We ought to obey God rather than man." Nevertheless, St. Paul is maintaining that, whatever particular mistakes or misdeeds rulers may commit, in fulfilling their general function of maintaining law by force they are serving God. This is the crucial question. For it is the State's use of force at all which is for some people's consciences the stumbling block; but it is that very point which is emphasized in the words: "He beareth not the sword in vain."

Let us begin by being quite clear that power is a thing neither to be admired and revered nor damned in itself. It is important to say that, because men are naturally inclined to worship power, or absolutely to condemn it. We are still restrained by our Christian teaching from professing such worship, though not always such condemnation. But as soon as vital Christianity disappears, men are openly told that they should sacrifice themselves for no other end than the increase of the power of the State, as though that were a good in itself.

The Christian teaching on this point is most definite.

"The Princes of the Gentiles exercise dominion over them and they that are great exercise authority upon them. But it shall not be so among you: but whosoever will be great among you, let him be your minister: and whosoever will be chief among you, let him be your servant: even as the Son of Man came not to be ministered unto but to minister, and to give his life a ransom for many."

That is the paradox about the State and its force. The commander, the ruler, the exerciser of force is justified only if he is acting as a servant. The force-using machinery of society must only be an instrument; it cannot, in spite of all its necessary pomp and power, be a primary thing. It is an instrument of the good life; a fence or wall to protect the real things which matter—the live, growing things—from being destroyed.

I had a letter in early August telling me that all the brussel sprouts and winter cabbage plants I had planted in July had been eaten by rabbits. The letter went on: "We are erecting a Siegfried Line of rabbit wire round the bed, and, when that is done, we can plant some more!" That homely illustration may help us to understand the real function of the State. How unlike to beautiful, live, growing things are rabbit wire and barbed wire and railings and walls! How much more constructive and creative it might seem to sow seeds and plant seedlings and bind up growing plants than to have to handle railings and barbed wire; but, as I was sadly reminded, unless you do the dull work of protection, the beautiful live things may just be destroyed. Where there are no railings, the only things which survive may be plants like gorse which grow their own prickles, or like bracken which no one wants to eat and which can become a pest. Observe, too—to expand the parable a little more—the nature of the protection you have to put up is dictated not by your sense of beauty or fitness, but by the nature of the attackers. No one in their senses would put up barbed wire for its own sake. It is nasty stuff. But there are some destroyers of the garden whom only barbed wire will deter.

There is an opposite point just as vital. It is possible to spend so much time on railings and barbed wire that you don't plant anything in the garden. There is almost nothing so desolate in the world as a plot of ground which has been thoroughly fenced off and protected in every way from the public with palings and barbed wire and glass bottles, and then left alone. It shouts: "Keep off." Not "Keep off" for the sake of the positive beauty growing inside, but just "Keep off." Only negation. That is to make negation, or the state of being undisturbed, an end in itself. That is to forget that protection is only justified by the living, growing value of what it protects. A Roman poet has a telling line about those who, in order to keep alive, lose everything which makes life worth living. The State that exalts power and force for its own sake is doing something like that. And we must remember that it is very difficult indeed to use power and not to abuse it. It is not enough to *say* that power is to be servant and not master. Unless arrangements are made to see that it is resisted when it tries to be master, things will certainly go wrong. As, with the complications of modern society, the State's powers tend to enlarge, the question becomes increasingly urgent.

Let me now apply the parable of the rabbit wire to the title of this chapter: "Church, State and Community." A Christian community should be permeated by the grace of our Lord Jesus Christ. Grace which goes beyond Law is, of its essence, free, spontaneous, overflowing. "The wind bloweth where it listeth. So is everyone that is born of the spirit." Therefore, in a Christian community, it will be recognized that the most valuable and precious things in the community cannot be prescribed, cannot be produced by law or rule or command. Prophets and poets and saints are not produced to order: yet it is a sign of a Christian community that prophets and poets and saints appear in it.

But Christian grace does not come out of anarchy or from isolated individuals. It grows in a fellowship. To be such a fellowship is the function of the Church. Of course the Church cannot help being an institution: it must have its rules and its organization; but its immediate and direct purpose in the life of the community is to be a fellowship in which grace is overflowing; where there is experiment and initiative; where more is done and given than the law requires or than conventional codes expect. There are fellowships like that. When you get inside them, you feel the exhilarating atmosphere. It is taken for granted that there are all sorts of exciting things which need doing, and the fellowship or some of its members are ready to tackle them. I hope we all know fellowships like that. Some of them are Churches, or connected with Churches, and some are not. Some organizations which call themselves Churches or congregations are, I am afraid, not at all like that. But a dead or half-alive Church is a sham and had better not exist. (See the message in Revelation to the angel of the Church of the Laodiceans.)

This atmosphere of life and spontaneity and fellowship cannot possibly be *created* by the State. That is not the State's business. The State's primary business is to see to the maintenance of such rules and order as will safeguard the free life of society which is carried on by all sorts of voluntary societies or organizations, of which Churches are only one conspicuous example. Because the State's rules have to apply to everybody, they can only lay down a minimum of behaviour—the minimum standard necessary to give everyone the security necessary for the best human relationships. Because no rules are any good as rules unless they are kept, the State has to enforce its rules. For an unruly society is a society where force reigns unchecked. For all the contrast between the Church and the State, for all the contrast between love and force, their functions, though different and to be distinguished, are, in a healthy community, complementary. For, if we have towards other people the active love which characterized the good Samaritan, we must be prepared, as he was, to go beyond the rules; but we must wish that the rules had been kept and a cruel and criminal act prevented. We must also wish that there should be rules for the protection of everyone, and we must therefore be ready to maintain for others, as well as for ourselves, the framework of the State.

This is all very well, but in practice it is not an easy matter to ensure that power is only used as a servant, or to decide when it is a usurper to be opposed and not a servant to be obeyed. We must therefore consider the limits of our duty to obey the State.

III

"KEEPING CÆSAR IN HIS PLACE"

I have said that the functions of State and Church were distinct but complementary; that it was the business of the State, the organization with power behind it, to act as a protection for the free life of society, and of the Church to inspire that free life. But I also said that, just because the State has organized power, it is not an easy business to keep that power as a servant or instrument. We have to discuss how to keep Cæsar in his place.

It is a ticklish job—it is well to recognize how ticklish it is. We can't do without Cæsar. If the organized force behind law is destroyed, the best things in life are at the mercy of lawless force. Almost anything, though not quite anything, is better than anarchy. Cæsar is very apt to presume on that and say: "You complain of the things I do: if I didn't do them, I should be destroyed, and where would all the fine things you care about be then?" In saying that, Cæsar is sometimes right and sometimes wrong. Who is to judge?

The present time, for example, is bringing home to us this lesson: that government is so indispensable an instrument for the protection of the ultimate values of free human intercourse, that we must be prepared to give that instrument, if need be, all we have and are. We can only save our lives if we are prepared to lose them for the sake of the highest things in life, and we can only do that by being prepared, when need comes, to sacrifice all in the service of that instrument, the State. At a crisis like this, we give tremendous powers into the hands of the State, confident that we can take them back when the crisis is over.

Yes, but should we be convinced that we ought to do this

unless we were convinced that the cause for which we are fighting is just? There may be conditions worse than anarchy. I have known, in recent years, patriotic Germans who have held that the hold of evil men over their country was so strong that the only chance of their country's salvation was that it should be defeated in war. What a terrible thing to have to believe about the country that you love; and yet only a real patriot could have felt it a tragedy, as they were feeling it. It is the mean and selfish men, men incapable of patriotism, who put order and security before everything.

I heard someone say the other day that Marshal Pétain was convinced that if he did not ask for an armistice there would be a revolution, and that therefore he was right in doing what he did. Surely they judge wrongly who so judge. Surely those Frenchmen are right who say that that is to deny the spirit of France. There is something in France of immeasurable worth—what we mean by the spirit of France—that is more injured by a shameful surrender than by revolution. I heard a wise and patriotic Frenchman the other day explaining that the disaster which has overcome France was due to the decay of the revolutionary spirit. He meant that, once orders were given by those in authority, very few dared to disobey them, however much they disapproved of them. You cannot carry on a government without obeying orders. And yet apparently you cannot preserve all that a government stands for without being prepared sometimes to disobey orders—without keeping an independent judgment.

In peacetime, our problem is comparatively simple, because we have a margin to play with. We know that embarrassing the government will not do very much harm. Therefore we can take into account the fact that, though government is indispensable, its agents are imperfect beings like ourselves and make mistakes, give orders which should not be given, use their powers to suppress criticism when they ought to welcome it, and so on. We recognize that power (particularly uncriticized power) has a bad effect on those who wield it.

A democratic State like our own recognizes this and provides means and opportunities for criticizing the executive. That, indeed, is what a democratic form of government essentially is—an organization of government to provide that the executive shall be sensitive to the criticism of those it is intended to serve. Even with good governments, the price of liberty is eternal vigilance. There is a natural tendency in government and administration to lay undue stress on routine and rules and proper channels and "in due course"—what is known by those who dislike it as red tape. Read Dickens' account of the Circumlocution Office in "Little Dorrit," which is, like most of Dickens' satire, both exaggerated and salutary. Even in peacetime, Cæsar needs to be kept in his place, but he can be so kept in a democratic country if there is a free and active social life, if Churches and other voluntary associations are alive. Cæsar grumbles and sulks a little; says, "If only the public would cease pestering me with these silly questions, I could get on with my job of serving the country," and produces a Parliamentary answer which explains at one and the same time that Cæsar's action has been impeccable and that all the same he will see it does not occur again. In times of crisis this problem is harder. For there is no margin to play with, and in a crisis every private judgment should be relentlessly purged because of the danger of caprice and self-seeking.

That is all ordinary democratic politics. Something much more serious is at issue when the State, even the democratic State, does plain evil. But it is important to understand what we mean by doing plain evil. We do not mean by it the State's action falling short of the highest standard of Christian perfection. We have no right to ask a government to act according to the highest standard of Christian perfection unless we know that the great mass of citizens are prepared so to act and to abide the consequences—and we know that they are not. No one has a right to be generous with other people's money or to commit other people to actions, however noble, which are against their will. A government's rules and actions cannot go much beyond the ordinary standard of decent behaviour of its citizens. If it disregards that standard, the only result is hypocrisy or disaster.

But there is, at any time, a certain standard of decent behaviour which most men expect of their country. A keen patriot ought to feel it like a wound when his country does something that is unworthy of its avowed standard of behaviour, and it is our duty to try to keep our country up to the principles it has professed, and be very jealous of our country's good name. To do this needs both courage and wisdom. When the Churches, or their representatives, take upon themselves this prophetic office and remonstrate with the government, they are commonly told that if they knew, as only the government does, the full circumstances of the case, they would have approved of what they now condemn. I think that is sometimes true and often quite untrue.

We may get very indignant over something we have misunderstood. The work of a prophet in modern times needs knowledge as well as moral principle. It is a hard enough task in peacetime; in the crisis which war produces, a much harder and more responsible job. For there are no rules for prophesying—only that a man should have eyes to discern between evil and good, and courage to follow what he sees. For when men take on themselves the rôle of a prophet, they do so at their peril. They will have no rules to assure them that they are right, and no public approval— only their own conviction. But, for all that, for all human fallibility, no society can afford to do without prophets. Without vision the people perisheth. Inspiration is often disturbing, but the best running machinery will not enable us to do without it. Without it we cannot keep Cæsar in his place.

I have left to the last a most serious problem, the conflict which arises when men are convinced that they must protest—not against the action of their government, but against the moral attitude of the great majority of their countrymen. Such conflicts do occur. The voice of the people is not the voice of God. Most moral reforms are brought about by pioneers who stand up against the accepted morals of their time. "Your fathers slew the prophets, but ye build their tombs" is a reproach which might be addressed to all generations.

The first men who protested against slavery were pioneers of this kind and suffered as such pioneers usually do.

I know from personal acquaintance and from my correspondence that many pacifists consider that, at the present time, they are moral pioneers standing up for a vision of

God's will not yet acknowledged by the majority of people. I do not myself agree. I think pacifists are, as prophets, false prophets. Yet I do not propose to argue about that, but to say this about the conflict: This is a conflict between different views of what is the will of God, and both sides of the conflict must act up to their lights and at least respect one another's sincerity. When a conflict of this kind does arise, it is bound to make both sides, majority and minority, search their hearts and consciences, apply to themselves that word of Cromwell's to the obstinate ministers of Scotland, "I beseech you, in the bowels of Christ, think it possible that you may be mistaken." If, after doing that, the conflict remains, it remains one of those tragic conflicts for which there is no immediate solution.

As Dr. Johnson said, when Boswell asked him about the early Christian martyrs: "The State had a right to martyr the early Christians and they had a right to be martyred." That is a hard saying, but there is something in it. As all Christians are called to be saints, so they are also in their degree called to be prophets. They will love and serve their own institutions, but they will not be conformed to the fashion of the age, and there will always be tension between the Christian conscience and the general standard of the community. If the Church ceases to arouse the community she serves, she fails in her function. Anyone who deeply feels a prophetic mission laid upon him must follow his conscience, even if that means that he must go against the great majority of his fellows and the State. But no true prophet will do that with complacency or without heartsearching; or indeed without an increasing determination not to stand above and apart from his fellows, but to be more than ever the servant of all.

The Church's Rôle in Politics

by

A. H. MURRAY and M. VERSFELD

Department of Ethics, University of Cape Town

When the Conference on Christian Reconstruction was held in South Africa in July, 1942, I was asked to contribute a paper on "The Distribution of Wealth and Property in a Christian State." It soon became clear to me that there was little one could say about this matter in any final sense from the Christian standpoint, for "wealth" and "property" are functional terms which change their meaning as the theory of society changes. The question really involved the further questions of the adaptation of the State to Christian ethics and of the methods to be used to make a Christian ethic prevail in the community and the State.

The reports from Study Circles which preceded the Conference showed the need of information on matters of political science. This lack accounts, I believe, for the general impression of futility which much contemporary writing on Church and State makes. In the daily life of the community the practical effect of this has been that a great deal of valuable will-power has been left without guidance or co-ordination, and so dispersed.

I was very fortunately able to get the help of Dr. Versfeld who contributes the third paper, on the Christian categories, under the title "The Material." The reader will be no less thankful to him than I am for the clarity and genuine profundity with which he completes that side of the argument.

A. H. M.

I

THE DEBRIS

RECONSTRUCTION does not happen in a void. Debris must usually be cleared away before the rebuilding can begin. Sometimes some part of the debris may be utilized in the new erection. This is the case particularly in the modern State, which was built up during four centuries on the materials of humanism, liberalism and the scientific method. Our examination of the debris will show that the menace to the social structure which safeguards our values consists in the maladjustment of the forces and tensions between the religious-ethical, humanistic, liberal and scientific elements with which our society is constructed. A new equilibrium between these forces must be found.

The early modern period starts well enough with humanism and liberalism holding out great promises for the future. Humanism was the fulfilment and fruition of the rich experience and scholarship of the Middle Ages; it also marked a change of emphasis in man's outlook. Perhaps it is more correct to say that humanism indicated a broader outlook than had been prevalent in the preceding periods. It included man and his nature in a more direct way and it took care to assert man's interests after a philosophical period which had erred on the side of theocentrism. The concept of humanism is not antithetic to religion, and early humanism was not even non-religious. Professor Luigi Sturzo has written: "It is one of the most common distortions of our attitude towards history, and one of the hardest to correct, to look upon humanism as the negation of the Middle Ages." That this is so appears very clearly in early humanist psychology, which kept to the sound tradition of medieval psychology. Humanism still regarded man as a whole and had not yet desiccated him into reaction-units by means of the categories of an uncritically accepted mechanistic psychology, as we moderns do.

Early humanism was able to surpass even the Aristotelian concept of man which made his reason his peculiar characteristic; for those people man was more; he could transcend himself, for he had a soul—a conception for which no place can be found in contemporary psychology, but in support of which the medieval mind could produce empirical evidence. Man was also a person. That meant that he was not merely the product of his environment and his heredity, but a thing-in-himself, a value by himself, not to be invaded by man or State, and free according to his own specifications. And the obvious fact of a dichotomy between evil and good in the soul of man was given recognition by the early humanists, following their immediate predecessors. This dichotomy was given deeper significance than it has to-day. It was made part of universal history and gave status and meaning to suffering and punishment. These were not interpreted in terms of the mechanism of social adjustment or libidinal liberation, when there is no standard of what adjustment is, or liberation. The humanists of the time were able to benefit by the sound psychology of the medievals while at the same time feeling the promise of "the new method" advocated by the scientists. The soft light of God's grace still threw a gentle radiance over the present. While living in the glow of the past men beheld the glory of the future.

The time when humanistic psychology would lose the categories of stability and self-containedness and identity—and thereby the basis of Christian ethics—to the concepts of adaptation, preservation, function and relation was still to come. The significance of the change-over from the one set of psychological categories to the other is the significance of modern history. Jacques Maritain has pointed out very truly that the trouble with our modern outlook is not its humanism, but the anthropocentrism and mechanism of the humanism. I think we may go further than this. When man lost the realist psychology of the Middle Ages and began to apply the abstractions of scientific categories to himself he was exposing himself to a further danger, that of naturalism. The danger has to a considerable extent become actual; anthropocentric humanism marks a stage in this development. To-day man is not even anthropocentric in his outlook; he is merely functional, proud to be a cog in a productive machine which produces—what? History without significance.

The force which falsified the promise of the early modern period and gave humanism and liberalism the lie we have called naturalism. Naturalism is really the habit of mind of the lazy thinker. It is the habit of seeing human beings and spiritual experiences, such as beauty and goodness, on a par with physical things. It is a lazy habit of mind because it refuses to answer questions which stare it in the face; for example, it is inclined to identify social success with "good" action and will not face the obvious fact that really good action is often not of the kind that leads to social success. The discoveries made by modern scientific methods and their application to the increase of man's worldly goods have now also promoted a demand for mechanical efficiency in man's human relations. This in turn has promoted the naturalistic or physicistic outlook in the philosophy of the popular mind. With the prevailing educational psychology, it is not possible to produce humanists. At universities the student is trained to perform some function to earn his living. He is carefully safeguarded from asking fundamental humanistic questions about the why and wherefore of things, or about the difference between good and bad, right and wrong, or about himself. Since all his time is taken up with his training, he naturally sees things and their meaning in the light of that particular subject. The schoolmaster is told that the purpose of his job is to adapt the child to society. To what end, we are not told, for that question is beyond the scope of the lazy naturalistic mind. If it were asked it would be seen that society is itself ever an instrument working for some further end—to-day the production of material goods and physical force.[1]

The third historical material which is found twisted up with humanism and naturalism among the debris and which is significant for our reconstruction is that of liberalism. We may describe liberalism as humanism applied to the spheres of economics and politics. It first made itself felt as the action of commerce to liberate itself from conservative institutions, particularly those of the political State and the institutionalized Church. The insufficiency of the outworn social forms of the medieval dispensation and the consequent growth of humanism promoted liberal action in economic and political spheres. So liberalism comes to stand for freedom of action and for freedom of the individual. It is clear that it presupposes an ethic of mutual understanding and trust, otherwise individual action can lead only to a state of war of all against all. So liberalism presupposes humanism and promotes it. But its fear of authority and tradition is so great that it is apt to develop a faint scepticism; it too often will not assert itself for fear of dominating the other person; for historic reasons liberalism usually takes up a negative attitude to social action; it is afraid to be an impediment to freedom. If it had not been for the super-liberalism of liberalism, it

[1] I have dealt more fully with this in my book on "The Philosophy of James Ward," Cambridge, 1937. (A. H. M.)

together with humanism might between them have staved off the onslaught of naturalism.

But as with humanism, the early great promise of liberalism is failing, and, as with humanism, the lack of fulfilment is due to the workings of naturalism. Liberalism succumbed, first, to capitalism and then, through industrialism and technological development, to naturalism. So it very soon contradicted its own professions. As open markets became fewer and competition keener, the groups who had promoted liberalism in the earlier stages in order to be free of social controls forgot their erstwhile liberalism and ran for protection to the very State against whose interference they had earlier protested. But they and the State had lost the guidance of the earlier Christian ethic—as the result of the working of naturalism on humanism. So now the guiding principle in the State was the profit-making spirit. Under liberalism the capitalist had freed himself, not only from the social control, but also from the ethics of the idea of a supreme end in life; in its honourable place was put the utilitarian ethic of profit. The substitution of a utilitarian ethic for liberalism lost the State for humanism, for humanism implies a spiritual ethic. With this gone, man's mind is open to impregnation by the outlook of naturalism; and then it is a simple matter to bring him under the subjection of Absolute Industrialism.

Let us not, however, be overcome with pessimism as we wander among the debris. What we have looked at are not the twisted remains of a humanism and liberalism which is now to be discarded and relegated to the pages of romantic history books. We have to do with an historical situation, which means that the forces we deal with may stretch far back and extend far forward. Some of this debris may still be useful when it has been adapted to suit the new situation, for it is of the stuff of human values. Nor does the fact that our starting point has been the Middle Ages mean that we must go back in retrogression. The new situation will not demand, for instance, the domination of a religious orthodoxy, as moderns fear, and some conservative Catholics and Calvinists demand. The Middle Ages happen to have possessed values to which our society has become insensitive and which have to be restored. What is necessary is a reassertion of the humanism and liberalism which came out of the Middle Ages. On this point T. S. Eliot has written some wise words, with which we may conclude our examination of the debris:

"It must be clear that I do not mean by a Christian State one in which rulers are chosen because of their qualifications, still less their eminence, as Christians. . . . I do not deny that some advantages may accrue from persons in authority, in a Christian State, being Christians. . . . But even if *all* persons in positions of the highest authority were devout and orthodox Christians, we should not expect to see very much difference in the conduct of affairs. The Christian and the unbeliever do not, and cannot, behave very differently in the exercise of office, for it is the general ethos of the people they have to govern, not their piety, that determines the behaviour of the politicians. . . . It is not primarily Christianity of the Statesmen that matters, but their being confined by the temper and traditions of the people which they rule, to a Christian framework within which to realize their ambitions and advance the prosperity and prestige of their country. They may frequently perform un-Christian acts, they must never attempt to defend their actions on un-Christian principles. . . . I should not expect the rulers of a Christian State to be philosophers . . . but they would have received a Christian education. The purpose of a Christian education would not be merely to make men and women pious Christians: a system which aimed too rigidly at this end alone would become obscurantist only. A Christian education would primarily train people to be able to think in Christian categories, though it could not compel belief and would not impose the necessity for the sincere profession of belief. What the rulers believed would be less important than the beliefs to which they would be obliged to conform. And a sceptical or indifferent statesman, working within a Christian frame, might be more effective than a devout Christian statesman obliged to conform to a secular frame. For he would be required to design his policy for the government of a Christian Society" ("Idea of a Christian Society," pp. 26–8).

The restoration of a Christian ethic of humanism and liberalism does not need an historical retrogression, nor revolutionary political activism. What is necessary is that the Christian-feeling public should become aware of the categories of their experience and then should decide, consciously, to assert these categories in their society.

II

THE SITE

The site on which the debris has to be sifted and cleared and the reconstruction executed is the State. It is not necessary for us to go into the theories of the future of the State. But we have to be clearly aware of those characteristics of the State which affect a Christian ethic, so that we may be able to devise ways and means by which that very self-conscious and specified entity called the Church may perform its social function. For the State is the instrument through which Society is approached, manipulated and regulated to-day.

Changes in modern society have been so rapid, and its present condition is so formless, that the term "the State" has about as many meanings as there are political theorists. For the lawyer, the State is the sovereign body wielding final authority; for the political theorists, "sovereignty" is a belated fiction; for the democrat, the State is the instrument by which the "people" execute their will; for the psychologist, there is no such thing as "the people"; for the political pluralist, the State is that function in the territory which regulates relations between all the other functions; for the monist, the State is the spirit permeating those functions. For our purpose, we may describe the State in terms of those qualities which affect the function of the Church more particularly. There are four such qualities.

The first characteristic is that *the modern State is a secular State*. We need not go into the history of the concept of the secular State, illuminating as this history is for the present situation. To-day the idea of the secular State has a two-fold significance for the Church which wishes to make a Christian ethic prevail in society. The one is that the State is neutral in relation to questions of value. The only value on which it takes a positive stand is that of self-preservation. For the rest, as regards ways and means, the interpretation of progress, of public welfare, of the good life, and so forth, the State maintains a neutral, and indeed, almost a careless attitude. It says in effect to its population: you decide among yourselves what you mean by these terms and then use me to promote your purpose. And if you cannot agree among yourselves, I will try to maintain a balance between your views. But it is for you to have the views and the values. The State regards its task as being prescribed by the people. This in fact means that it is prescribed by the group which knows how to seize power. The appeal of the State is not to any absolute standard of values, beyond that of self-preservation and neutrality. Actually it is there to be used by those who know how.

The second relevant quality of the contemporary State is closely associated with the first. *The Modern State is a naturalistic State*. This is so both in fact as well as in the minds of men. The contemporary approach to political philosophy is no longer through ethics, as it was for the Greeks, or through theology, as it was for the medievals, but assumes a particular method and calls itself Political Science. Now, science describes and does not prescribe, and its method is intended only to aid observation; it offers no standards of values, nor any theory of purpose, nor can it give any significance to anything. That is the reason, I think, why one finds so little illumination from this science, or its younger sisters, psychology and sociology, in the study of the phenomena of the State. In public speeches and in the Press we are told *ad nauseam* that politics is economics. In effect, to say that politics is economics is to say that the modern State is naturalist, which is to say that it submits to the natural course of events like a phenomenon of Nature. It no longer, being the highest of all communities, "aims, and in a greater degree than any other, at the highest good," as Aristotle said. The machine aspect or administrative aspect of government activity is very much to the fore these days. And, being naturalistic, the State is not always aware of the forces which run the machine, nor of the purpose for which it is run.

In the third place, *the contemporary State is a liberal State*. This sounds far better than it really is, for liberalism, having become untrue to itself (as we saw a moment ago), is too often associated with ethical drabness. Liberalism has failed, temporarily, because it has not understood itself. In the popular mind liberalism means that I must not interfere with the other man's freedom of action. Thus understood all is well. Unfortunately, this attitude of mind emphasizes the belief that, in order not to dominate the other man, I may not assert my own convictions or express them either. So an ethically neutral and colourless social atmosphere is created. The next step in the liberal fallacy follows quickly. In this society it is easy to come to believe that I, being liberal, must not interfere with my own actions either; I must be free, "to do as I like." In an ethically neutral society all feeling for self-specification is quickly lost. But this is not liberalism: it is sheer drift. One has one's own best nature according to which one must live and communicate if oneself and an honestly liberal society are to survive. One cannot be a liberal with relation to oneself: one should be under the dictatorship of one's own best nature. One can be a liberal only in relation to the other man, and only for so long as he in turn observes the rules of the game of liberalism: to obey the demands of his own best nature. It is because the contemporary liberal has not realized the real nature nor the implications of his liberalism sufficiently clearly that his outlook is tinged with a drifting scepticism so that he cannot assert himself and the values of his liberalism. When this state of mind is reached it is easy enough for a self-assertive, positive, if unphilosophical outlook such as is engendered by profit-making industrialism to come to dominate the outlook of the age. If people are clear about their values and their outlook the liberal State is the soundest condition of spiritual and cultural growth. It is because the liberal State has not understood its own nature as an ethical-religious-humanistic growth out of the Middle Ages that it has drifted into naturalism, and thence into Absolute Industrialism.

The fourth characteristic of the State is *its industrialized nature*. I do not mean that the State runs or owns the numerous industries operating within its boundaries. I mean that the welfare and the policy of the State have become intimately bound up with the policy pursued by those industries. The very mind of man has taken on the habit of thinking in industrial terms. His outlook is one with that of industrial interests. He arranges his life's plan—and its ideals—according to the prescriptions of the industrial system. Now the State, as Plato said, is not made of oaks nor stones, but of the character of the people in it. The problems of the modern State are the problems of the contemporary property-mentality and the policy of the State is prescribed by the exigencies of the property-situation. The ethical implications of this are not yet realized. When the State demands of its schools that they should produce children who are able to take their place in society it means that it wants children to form cogs in the industrial machinery. That is a serious matter. For what of the child?

The quality of industrialism, the fourth relevant characteristic which is significant for our understanding of the place of a Christian ethic in the life of the State, is in many ways the antithesis of the earlier liberalism of the State. Liberalism is calculated to counteract any tendency to absolutism, mental, political or economic. Understood in the right way it is the condition of freedom. Unfortunately its inordinate fear of domination, and its naïve expectation that the other side will be equally liberal in its attitude, has too often made it neutral and ineffective in its approach. On the other hand industrialism is a rising force, knowing what it wants, with no neutrality about it. It is nothing if not positive. It is untrammelled by any awareness of its history and it lives only in the present. Thus it is able to ride rough-shod over the qualities which it shares with the State, the secularism, liberalism and naturalism, which are all the outcome of historical experience and development. Industrialism does not know the values of these things, for human values can often be understood only in the light of history; while the industrialist temper is innocent of appeal to anything which is not immediately present. Herein lies the menace of the "practical man." The industrialized State increasingly becomes the enemy of real man, even while promoting the amenities of his civilization. Occasionally it still echoes the language of ethics and of Christian thought when the antagonisms which it has created in human society become so unbearably opposed that it has to show that it is aware of them. But its attempts to alleviate the distress which it has caused among three-quarters of the world's population are of a purely expedient nature. It tries to "improve" the situation by a "better plan of distribution." It never has, for it cannot, ask itself the question: what does improvement mean? So it builds flats with the latest devices to promote creature comfort, and then refuses to let them to people with babies. But the industrialized State, in spite of its impracticable practicality and its unethical ethics, is yet unknowingly perpetuating an historic tradition. When the world was empty and real liberalism was the order of the day industrialism did not seek out the State. Indeed, it rather avoided the State and always exhorted the State to keep its place. But as the world became full and gentlemen's wars of conquest became national wars for markets, the industrialist sought out the State. He first wooed her and then embraced her, until to-day the State and its organ of expression, the Press, are fighting the battles of industrial interests. Indeed, the battles are themselves the battles of industrial competition. Industrialism uncriticized by humanism and liberalism has promoted power-politics which has gone from strength to strength, overriding man's claims to his health, his family, the holiness of his Sabbath, a liberal as opposed to a technical education, freedom of information and thought, in the course of its destructive growth.

The political theorist who studies the present State while keeping in mind its history—for the State is essentially historical as well as immediately present—must be impressed by the bearing of the four qualities which we have enumerated on a policy framed to assert an ethical view of things. He must also be impressed by the antithesis between secularism and liberalism on the one hand, and industrialism on the other. This antithesis will explain to him the hesitancy in contemporary political theory which does not seem to be able to present to him a bold outline of what the State is or should be; and it will explain to him the dichotomy in the life of the citizen. To-day the citizen does not know what to think of things. While he admires the great results of industrial efficiency everywhere, he feels its chains closing round him, and he fears for his freedom. This social and personal dichotomy, together with these qualities of the State, constitute the problem of the reconstruction of a Christian ethic on this site.

The political problem is to restore man to his rightful place in his earthly kingdom. The uncritical acceptance of the great blessings of science, scientific method and industrialism, has—as uncritical action is apt to have—also its negative side. This lies in the emphasis it has put on a mechanical outlook on things and the great pre-occupation with physical nature that it has promoted. So great has this pre-occupation become that naturalism is now a habit of mind and forms the unexamined premise for judgments of social values. This mental habit, combined with the demands of the industrial system on the individual, makes man physically and spiritually a cog in the social production machine. Not man's nature, but the demands of scientific production, prescribe ethical values. To restore man to himself the Church will have to explain liberalism to itself. It will have to point out that the scepticism which is characteristic of the liberal mind is in fact a denial of it. The greatness of liberalism is to enable man to be himself and to be specified according to his nature. When one appreciates one's own nature one will also appreciate the other man's nature and will grant him the opportunity to be what he naturally has in him to be. Liberalism is the quality of one's relation to others, not to oneself. The drifting sceptic has no need of liberalism; he has not got it in him to be a liberal.

Once liberalism has understood itself it will be found that the excessive naturalism to which the State has been prone will fall into its rightful place in the national philosophy. There are natural processes, also, in man's social relations. A realistic Church cannot deny real things. The point is to keep naturalism within its rightful limits and to break man of his materialistic pre-occupation. But there is all the difference in the world between submitting to the blind forces of nature—which in society are the forces of material production and their effects on the lives of men—and steering those forces to serve man in the light of some clear set of ethical values which are of man's own nature. The fact is that at present it is the scientist's mind which has all the external marks of the religious spirit: an intense enthusiasm, generous underpaid service to society, uncritical acceptance and generalization of so-called principles. A little philosophic criticism is usually enough to convince the scientist of the real limits of his genuine knowledge. Indeed, it is usually not the pukka scientist who falls a prey to naturalism, physical or social; it is the second-rate scientist and the journalistic scientist who propagate the foolish philosophy. When the Church has succeeded in restoring a balanced outlook in society by its rejuvenation of liberalism and humanism the citizen will become fully conscious of his own nature and self-specification. Then it will be easy to explain and maintain that naturalism only goes so far in explaining man and society and that the rest belongs to another realm, and that this is really the important realm of experience. What is needed, after all, is a return to the realism which many medievals had and which we seem to have lost, the psychology of spiritual man.

When these philosophic conditions have been attained the secularized State will perform its proper function almost automatically. I believe that the secular State is an important advance on previous stages of political development. It offers the best opportunity for humanism and liberalism and the best safeguard against absolutism, spiritual, economic or political. But it only offers this safeguard if a real secularity is maintained by the activity of the real human in its territory, and it does not become naturalistic or economic or fall into some other kind of particularity. The function of the State is an expedient function in an historical, and therefore expedient, situation. But care must be taken that the forces which act through the State, and use the instrumentality of the State, are ethical forces, and not the blind forces of economic nature. Man has two sides to his nature, the universal, or, as the religious mind has it, the eternal side, and the material or expedient or economic aspect. In so far as he is in touch with the State he is moving in expedient spheres. But he is still fully human. The secularism of the State must be a humanized secularism, not a materialistic secularism.

It is when liberalism has been helped by a Christian ethic to become real liberalism, and is no longer confused with scepticism and neutrality; when economic materialism has been taught its rightful place in the scheme of things and no longer poses as a universal philosophy; and when secularism has found its rightful inspiration in humanism; that we can expect to reap the full blessings of modern productive technique. The restoration of the balance is the task of the Christian Church. If once a religious humanism as we described it above is maintained it will not matter greatly what the relation between the State and industry is. Real humanism will maintain itself in social conditions which may range from the extremes of individualism and *laissez-faire* to the opposite pole of State ownership of the instruments of production. The choice of the economic system is the selection of the make of machine you require: under some conditions American cars serve better, under others British; the home-made product is usually the best adapted, however, especially in things of the mind. But it is real humanism which must be at the wheel. Then industry will produce power, but not power-politics; class conflict will make place for division of labour; and industry will of its own free will be kept within its rightful limits, which is in the realm of the expedient in human nature, and will not encroach on real life.

As earlier, when we examined the debris of the present situation, our conclusion now, after we have looked over the site, is again that our problem is essentially one of restoration—adapted to new conditions, of course. We have seen that the site offers incidental advantages when once the debris has been sifted and cleared; history has not been in vain these last three hundred years. It does not appear that a revolution in any exhaustive sense of the word is necessary. Personally I doubt whether the logic of man's mind works by means of revolutions; real man is internally too coherent and integrated for that. What is necessary is that politics should be freed from naturalism, and more particularly from the naturalism of economics, and restored to ethics—the position to which the medieval mind had attained and which we have since lost.

III

THE MATERIAL

How nominal the Christian character of our society is becomes clear as soon as we ask those whom we meet even the most elementary questions about the Christian Faith. Even those who come from a Christian environment hold their Christianity merely as a vague sentiment, and are quite inarticulate about its dogmas. The notions of "grace," "atonement," "incarnation," "original sin" have dropped out of the popular mind. This indicates not merely a lack of interest in the Christian faith, but a lack of good history teachers in our schools, from whose lips no word escapes about the great ideas which patterned our civilization. As a sociological phenomenon, popular indifference to dogma must be attributed largely to the divorce between religion and morality which took place in the nineteenth century under the weight of rationalist criticism. It was then thought possible to preserve Christianity as an ethical code while rejecting the supernatural elements. The emphasis then came to be thrown upon action rather than belief. "Being a Christian" came to mean in effect accepting current notions of altruism, liberalism, benevolence, honesty and kindliness, and consoling oneself with the thought that the practice of these constituted the whole duty of a Christian.

The consequences have been nothing less than disastrous for Christianity. So poorly did rationalism serve to free the human mind of its need for dogma that into the house thus swept and garnished entered the diabolical crew of emotional, secular and political faiths which constitute the religion of modern man. In a study devoted to Christian Action it is imperative to call attention to the dangers of Christian Activism, and of *soi-disant* Christian political, social and economic programmes divorced from Christian philosophy, Christian faith, and Christian mysticism. The reader could do worse than to read, in this connection, the chapter on Politics and Religion in Mr. Aldous Huxley's "Grey Eminence." Christian Action can easily become a mechanism of escape for those who have forgotten what manner of spirit they are.

In an activistic age calling for reforms, new orders, active intervention within the social field, it is as necessary as it may be unpopular to call a halt and ask Christians first to take stock of themselves. If their intervention on the social plane is to be effective, they must first remember that they are not primarily citizens of the world in which that action takes place. Christianity is not primarily a moral or an ethical code, but a faith in a supernatural order. The whole being of a Christian is centred in a life which escapes complete realization within the framework of space and time. The presupposition of all Christian Action is the recognition that the ultimate beatitude is not to be enjoyed in this life. The central insight of Christian Action must be that it can only hope for success in so far as it recognizes the necessarily transient and approximate character of its achievement. This tends to be overlooked, and Christians to associate themselves with certain purely secular millenarian movements because the notion of the Kingdom of God on earth is reached by materializing the eternal rather than transfiguring the temporal. The advent of the Kingdom means the consummation of history, not its prolongation.

The fundamental metaphysical characteristic of a Christian is, then, that he is a member of the *Civitas Dei*. His first duties are not ethical nor political, but religious. The core of his life is his relation to God. His primary activities are the activities of prayer and worship. All his secular rights and duties, all his political and economic arrangements, must be orientated towards and reflexively transformed by these activities. They must both conserve him in and point him out of this world, *and only in so far as they succeed in the latter do they succeed in the former*. They are themselves conserved in so far as there has crept into their structure the pattern of things not seen. That to seek first the Kingdom of God is the only way to preserve things temporal, that concentration upon the latter evaporates them, has been the theme of Christian philosophers of history from Augustine to Dr. A. J. Toynbee. Hence it is easy but untrue to say that the Christian is not concerned with the problems of this world, though he knows that the principles of their solution cannot be naturalistic. Furthermore, he does not even regard natural things as mere *means* to his supernatural end. They are in themselves and in a relative way good and worthy of love, being made in their degree in the image of God. "It is plain that neither necessity nor use, but only his mere will moved God to make what was made, that is 'Because it was good': which was said after it was done, to show the correspondence of the good creature to the Creator by reason of whose goodness it was made. If this Goodness be now the Holy Spirit, then is all the whole Trinity intimate to us in every creature" (Aug., "de Civ. Dei," XI : 24).

The great opportunity which this time of scepticism and disintegration offers to the Christian is to rethink his position in the light of fundamental dogmas. He cannot accept his way of life from a social atmosphere which is so obviously not Christian. This is an age in which to be a Christian means to swim against the stream, and the independence of mind to achieve this feat can be achieved only by a return to dogma. Nothing in our own time has been more misrepresented and misunderstood than the nature of dogma, whose function properly understood is to free our lives from slavery to temporary social fashions, and our minds from irrational influences. If we want to think in a Christian way, for instance, in the sphere of social relations we must think out, and feel out, our position from the intellectual and emotional contents of the dogmas of the Creation and the Incarnation.

I have thus far emphasized the supernatural orientation of Christians. But, except in times and places of deterioration, Christian thought has not placed an impassable gap between Nature and supernature. It has regarded the supernatural as the perfection of the natural, and the natural as the analogy of the supernatural. While the dogmas both of the Creation and the Incarnation call to mind primarily the transcendence of God, they also give a positive significance to Nature and to history. They prevent the Christian from regarding the world of Nature and of human society as barren of intrinsic worth, at the same time that they prevent him from attributing to them an absolute worth. If God made the world in His own image then it is good. If He was incarnate in history, then the historical process becomes a spiritual reality and not merely a witness to the transience and insignificance of the things which are made. Underneath its changing structure there is revealed an order which abides, and of which all things in their degree are a witness. It is on the question of the importance of the historical that the Christian parts company with the Manichee and the Buddhist.

If the Incarnation then is a revelation of the eternal it also gives a new significance to the body and the temporal. It was the resurrection of the *body* which was one of the most striking notes in the new spirituality. The sense of the relevance of body to spirit and of spirit to body is essential to the Christian mind, which is essentially a sacramental mind. Man is a whole of body and mind. It is by bodily things that his own spirit is aroused, and by which he arouses the minds of others. We can express the faith that is in us only in action through and upon matter. I can communicate my thoughts to you only by means of vibrations in the air, or marks on paper. Pure spirits do not need books or gramophone records. History itself cannot be recaptured without the material vestiges and monuments which it has left behind, and on the durability of matter depends the capacity of man to look before and behind. Nothing more truly expresses the mind of Christ than his sympathy with the bodily needs of men. He turned water into wine to make a marriage more festive.

Thus it seems a clear demand of Christianity itself that it shall concern itself deeply with the forms of society, and with the æsthetic and economic sides of life. But instead of external puritanic or doctrinaire or political meddling with these it is committed to their transformation by the persuasion of its inner freedom, sympathy and joy. There is the closest connection between the forms of our community and consequently of the structure of the minds within it, and the way in which its farmers, engineers and artists deal with the raw material of Nature. I mention the artist because after the Middle Ages the æsthetic implications of Christianity have been so largely forgotten. The city, writes Mr. Lewis Mumford in the Introduction to his "Culture of Cities," "is a conscious work of art—mind *takes form* in the city, and in turn, urban forms condition mind. For space, no less than time, is artfully reorganized in cities: in boundary lines and silhouettes, in the fixing of horizontal planes and vertical peaks, in utilizing or denying the natural site, the city records the attitude of a culture and an epoch to the fundamental facts of its existence. The dome and the spire, the open avenue and the enclosed court, tell the story, not merely of different physical accommodations, but of essentially different conceptions of man's destiny. With language itself, it remains man's greatest work of art." And elsewhere he remarks that the daily education of the senses is the groundwork of all higher forms of education. There is a connection between Christianity and, for instance, town-planning and public works, other than a purely economic one. The ugliness of our cities is the measure of our lack of faith, and a very real hindrance to inspiring it. Insistence on public beauty is a crying Christian duty and not a subordinate one. And there is absolutely no need for this beauty to take conventional or orthodox forms. The only beauty which is Christian is simply beauty.

A Christian, then, is a man who is aware of his supernatural destiny, and aware of his duty to organize the world of space and time in the light of this end. In doing so he has to remember that both he, and the materials which he uses, are in their degree made in the image of a God who is a *creator*. Since man is conscious of his nature, it is his duty consciously to create, that is, to bring men and materials to their own proper perfection. Man as Christian is man as an active *maker*, a maker of good men and beautiful things. He has a passion for imaginative transformation, for making all men and all things new. God is Himself the unmoved Mover, but He sets all things in motion, and the contemplation of God does not freeze men into a passive immobility, which is a caricature of His rest, but moves them to an everchanging activity which is the true imitation of Him. He who desires to create a Christian order must be willing to leave safety

41

behind, to make room for adventure both of the body and of the spirit. He must visualize a world in which men are imaginatively awake, and whose duty to each other is perhaps simply this, that they recognize in each other the power to make things new and provide each other with the tools and materials, both physical and spiritual, for the private adventure of being a man.

The consequence of this sense of the self-sufficiency of God is for the Christian a sense of the insufficiency and incompleteness of created things together with a sense of their active gravitation towards the divine. Together with a sense of the relativity of his works of art, and of his ideas of personal and social excellence, goes an appreciation of the beauty and significance in which all participate. His stimulus to change, his sense of the relative, derive from his sense of the *analogous* character of created things, and of the One Abiding whose image they are, and Who always calls out new forms from the active insufficiency of finite things.

Hence together with a sense of order there must always be a kind of inspired anarchy in a Christian community. Creation, the fruit of real life, is unpredictable, and a social order which implies that what a man does is completely foreknowable and provided for cannot be a Christian order. The Christian life and the Christian community must be a system of fruitful tensions, of high hope, of faith in the reasonableness of what is in the Pauline sense the foolish. It is a life which lives dangerously because it knows that there only does its safety lie. Only by risking spectacular failure does it survive. To put it differently, the virtue of charity, that is, the habit of imaginative sympathy, takes new forms, gives a shock of surprise, with every occasion of its exercise. As soon as we legalize it, ossify it into a set of well defined obligatory duties, then necessary as the latter may be as an educative substructure, we have taken the leaven out of the community's life. No community whose members pray and make really useful and beautiful things can ever be contented to remain as it is. It will be traditional because its tradition is a tale of new things and a source of new actions.

Hence, there can in a sense be no such thing as a Christian

42

State or a Christian Order, if we understand by these a system of spatial and temporal arrangements taken as absolute and fixed by law and custom. There can be a Christian State if we conceive of it dynamically, as a *system of opportunities* which define themselves in the course of its life, and readjust their means as the opportunities are taken, in order to secure new imaginative releases. A Christian State will ask itself one prime question: what do men require to do and make things, since doing and making are holy, though only when they spring out of the will of the man himself? It will not delude itself with absolutist or millenarian dreams. It will not try to stifle all tension and difference, but will provide a framework within which they can find that expression which is the necessary preparation for a new synthesis. It must provide adequate organs for the powers which it releases to play upon itself and adjust it to their needs, for they are the ends of which it is but the instrument. A Christian order is but a thing of the earth, relative, imperfect and perishable, which perhaps must die to bring forth its fruits. It shall wax old as doth a garment. Humble in its mortality, it can bear witness to the life from which it comes and to which it points. Idolized as an absolute, regarded as the Kingdom of God on earth, it will become, it cannot but become, the consummation of all tyrannies.

IV

WAYS AND MEANS

The problem of the relation between Church and State is many centuries old. The situation will always contain the possibilities of friction, for it expresses one of the primary dichotomies of man's natural nature. Political problems are not solved, in any final sense of the term. What has to be done is to find a balance between the forces which make out the antithesis. We have criticized writers on the problem of Church and State for not describing the nature of the State or its machinery in their presentation; in this way the State has remained a vague concept in the mind of the layman, and the attitude of the Church member to it unrealistic. Because of this one-sidedness, writers who approach the matter from the Church's point of view are apt to look helplessly to the past, and to do nothing about the present except to lament its secularism, its naturalism, its liberalism and its industrialism. Among extreme conservatives in both the Roman and the Calvinist tradition there is a tendency to contrast the early "Church" State with the "liberal" State of the nineteenth century and its results to-day. We are then told that man has become enslaved to forces which annihilate his spiritual freedom and, indeed, his very existence; by way of example, it is pointed out that to maintain a Christian order man has to obey a State which, to sustain itself and the Christian order, makes un-Christian demands on him. Reference may then be made to the increasing interference by the State in the life of the individual, and it may be pointed out that this interference is increasingly utilitarian and anti-individual in its incidence. And so, we are told, we live in the shadow of the menace of the State.

It has been our interpretation of political development that the modern State need constitute no threat and need contain no menace to the ethical ideals and strivings of Christian man which are still expressed in the humanistic and liberal tradition which has its roots in the Middle Ages. We have indicated how this historic material of our civilization has become warped and distorted by the force of a misapplied scientific method leading to a false philosophy called naturalism. But we have suggested that historical forces have on the whole promoted a concept of the State which, if rightly understood, not only is not anti-man, but may pave the way for the ideal to which our humanism and liberalism points, that of a religious humanism. It has been our argument to show that neither the contemporary State—with its secular, liberal, naturalistic and industrial aspects—nor its machinery need operate against the maintenance of a Christian ethic. And we ventured to suggest what were some of the categories of a Christian theory of life.

All this does not exclude the possibility of conflict between Church and State. We have said that in a political situation we are concerned with a balance and not with a final solution.

Dr. Henry Emerson Fosdick has described the problems which the present historic and expedient situation has created for religion as follows:—

"In at least four major realms religion is feeling the powerful impact of the world's disturbed condition. First, the modern intellectual upheaval has shattered the mental pattern in which religion historically has been set. Second, religion, inevitably adding a sense of sacredness to everything it touches, has made holy many moral codes and customs which rapidly changing conditions have outmoded, so that religion's ethical leadership is widely doubted and challenged. Third, religion finds itself desperately at odds with opposing social philosophies. Under capitalism its ethic of love is denied the overwhelming dominance of the profit-motive; under communism it is outlawed as an enemy of the State; under fascism and nazi-ism it is both refused freedom of action and utterance within the nation and is denied a universal God. Fourth, all the religions of the earth are increasingly poured together in the mixing-bowl, with resultant cohesions and collisions, recognitions of kinship and of difference, infinitely disturbing—and promising." (I owe this passage to Rhyllis Alexander Goslin, "Church and State," Foreign Policy Association.)

In South Africa the dichotomy has not yet developed to this extreme form; in this country the two main factors which are anti-Christian in their incidence on social life are the naturalistic outlook (of which most people are unconscious), and the maldistribution of property and property rights (of which we have become increasingly aware of latter years). It is possible that these tendencies may develop to the point that they dominate the State, thus engendering a real conflict between Church and State. In such a world humanism and liberalism will have ceased and the realistic Church will have to maintain the purity of its heart by withdrawal, even by isolation. In our world, however, liberalism and humansim still are active and potent. While that is the case the conflict may be potential but is not, and need not become, actual.

In the contemporary State the Church which maintains

its aloofness to preserve its purity can exercise its social and political function in two ways. The first is that of criticism; the other, participation by its members in the political and government machinery.

Criticism

Democracy is a precious thing and its machinery is fragile. Many descriptions and criticisms of democracy remind one of nothing so much as of the proverbial bull in the crockery trade. The essence of democracy, and that upon which the values which its guarantees and promotes rests, is intelligent criticism. In the course of man's struggle for rights, privileges and Right, the democratic procedure of criticism has developed into a fine art with rules of its own which are observed in parliament and in all public discussions. A great modern English philosopher, Bernard Bosanquet, has described the process and life of the modern free State in the term "operative criticism." It is to the extent that mind meets mind and clashes freely with mind that common solutions on an advanced level are found. Democratic criticism is a process of creative discussion. In this process the Church must uphold its values and put its point of view. Democratic discussion goes on all the time anywhere and everywhere, in bars and canteens, private drawing-rooms and clubs, the Press, party caucus meetings and parliament. It is significant that the Church usually has some sound common-sense point of view to put forward on current problems. But somehow the ethical views of the Church on everyday problems are regarded as a specialist theory and people are not sufficiently well acquainted with them to recognize their value. That is because of the prevailing naturalistic habit of thought. Instead of criticizing the maladjustments of property for what they are, the outcome of a social system without ethics, the argument rushes into the ways and means offered by economics and it is forgotten that economic ways and means are but instruments of the good or bad will of people. As a useful analysis of this mentality we may take Professor Tawney's description of the value-judgments of contemporary society:

46

"Its emphasis on the supreme importance of material riches; its worship of power; its idealization not merely of particular property rights, but of property in general and as an absolute; its subordination of human beings to the exigencies, or supposed exigencies, of an economic system; its erection of divisions within the human family based, not on differences of personal quality or social function, but on differences of income and economic circumstance—these qualities are closely related to the ends which capitalist society hold to be all-important. In such societies, as the practice of the latter clearly shows, they are commonly regarded not as vices, but as virtues" (from 't Hooft and Oldham, "The Church and its Function in Society," Allen and Unwin, p. 210).

The criticism implied in this description is felt by the mass of the people, but they are at a loss how to argue about these phenomena. The same holds very largely for the unease that is felt about the social situation. This complex of problems is economic on top only; at bottom social relations are a matter for ethical analysis and action.

The required criticism is not a question of changing the laws of the State, nor of bewailing the badness of human nature nor the ethics of big business. It is a matter of expressing publicly a judgment on social action which happens but should not happen, whether the law allows it or not. The question here of primary importance is that of human values. The public of a secular State containing a considerable Christian community have the right to expect that the Christian trained in economics will publicize the facts. The modern phenomenon of big business needs continual ethical criticism, from the usage (which appeared frequently during the 1928–32 depression) of sacking employees because of bad business (but not at the same time decreasing the dividends paid to the shareholders) to the formation of monopolies to exploit the consuming public. The protection of ethical values in the democratic State does not involve State action in the first instance; its way of assertion is that of publicity. Within the present framework of legislation there is great opportunity for improvement, which the public must be made to see. In a democracy the way to do this is by continuous discussion and criticism. In this process the Church must assert its position. It must continually put before the public the facts of the case, and its ethical arguments on these facts. For it is the guardian of the ethical principles, and the nature of the social problem is essentially ethical.

The function of critical discussion in the operation of the contemporary democratic State appears very clearly if we study the place of the Press in affairs to-day. In his excellent Penguin volume on "The Press," Mr. Wickham Steed has said that the problem of the Press is the central problem of democracy. He indicates the new spirit of the Press which he believes is coming and which we may call the new seriousness in journalism, or, perhaps better, the spirit of scientific journalism. Mr. Calpin, writing about English-Afrikaans relations in South Africa, says: "The Press has become a serious factor in racial strife." For myself, I see no chance of harmonious race relations in South Africa, whether on the principle of conciliation or parallelism, without a serious reconsideration of the Press in politics. The Church which wants to maintain itself in present democracy will have to give very serious attention to the Press, both as regards the duties and functions of its own Press, and the ethics of the commercial Press. The time has come for it to consider promoting its own Press. The principles on which modern society is run are information and criticism, which implies the institutions of the Press. The private profit Press, however, has not in the past promoted real criticism, nor has it always offered the requisite information and opportunities for sound discussion; it too often has followed "interests" while pretending to guide the public. Because a superficial scientificism is current, the Press will play up anything that goes under the name of science, and will have little space for the consideration of ethical matters on which the society which it pretends to serve is founded. When a scientific society met in 1942, and incidentally made a number of insignificant remarks about science and society, the Press of the whole country afforded it reports of several columns daily. When at the same time a conference was held by united Churches of the country on Christian reconstruction, reports averaged six inches daily.

There is another sphere of social function which calls for the critical action of the Church. That is public education. There will be difference of opinion on this point among my readers. The traditionalists will say that education is the function of the Church. I believe, however, that under contemporary conditions the duty of the Church is to make itself felt in the educational curriculum to counteract the tendency to naturalism in educational theory. Control of education by the Church would, however, appear to be both undesirable from a theoretical point of view and impracticable. It is to be doubted whether an inculcated dogma will promote the spirit of real religious humansim. It may safely be taken that the modern State school has come to stay. The point that the Church must recognize is that the machinery is actually there to enable the Church to see that the spirit of religion is maintained in public educational institutions. Possibly the greatest error of our age, and one over which future scholarship will make merry greatly, is the practice known as "psychologism" and the attempt to explain the internal relations of mental and spiritual experience in terms of the simple, indeed, almost naïve, categories of the natural sciences. It is the task of a learned and critical Church to recognize and act on these matters, and to this end it is essential that those in authority consider raising the standards of training for their clergy very considerably to meet the case.

I do not think that the critical function of the Church in society can be left to run itself. For the criticism to be pertinent and effective it will be necessary to have bodies— more or less informal—the particular task of which it will be to be informed on these matters. Often the mere presence of such a body will be sufficient to prevent an undesirable action or development. Careful consideration, however, will have to be given to the best methods of promoting and publishing the criticism under various conditions. A particularly watchful eye will have to be kept on the Press, and deputations to editors, and when necessary to directors, will have to be the order of the day. Members of Parliament, of provincial councils and municipalities must also be watched and there should be no hesitation about arranging deputations or private interviews when these gentlemen talk or act against the principles of Christian ethics. The pulpit might once again resume its historic task of social criticism. More important than all that, however, and in keeping with the contemporary State, will be the local and provincial bodies set up by the Christian community to keep an eye on public action, and through which the Church will be able to act as a pressure group to assert itself with relation to the demands of other pressure groups.

Indirect Participation

The second method by which the Church is able to exercise its social function in the secular State is by the participation of its members in public activity. The Church itself remains separate and apart. Experience on the continent of Europe, for example with the Christian-Historical Party of Dr. Kuyper in the Netherlands, has taught the lesson that a profession of orthodoxy by a ruling party need not signify a Christian life in the State. And expression of opinion on contemporary affairs by the Church as such need not promote the just solution of a problem either. This appeared in the Dreyfus case in France and again during the recent civil war in Spain. The social problem with which the Church is concerned is always a particular here-now problem. But the Church meditates on it and finds the principles of the solution in seclusion, apart from considerations of expediency and practical exigencies. The Church is like the research worker. The nature of its social solution is experimental. It is constantly faced with new situations for which it has to find the right interpretation. The solution is actual and particular. But it is worked out in seclusion, as the scientist retires to his laboratory to find the correct formulæ to combat the raging disease.

Without directly participating in political and social issues the Church can still through its members keep a watchful eye on nominations for election to local, provincial and central bodies. The workability of the humanist, liberal

Christian State depends in the last instance on its numerous advisory, governing and administrative bodies, and I believe that the function of the Church is clear in this connection. The very fact that the Church shows a watchful eye will go a long way to attaining the desired end; active comment, even privately, on party nominations will be necessary only occasionally.

The citizen who regularly tries to apply a Christian ethic to public duties will sometimes find himself in difficulties; and more so now with the pressure-group State than at the time of the individualistic State. To-day political effect can only be achieved by group action. The citizen has to belong to a professional or trade union, a league or party caucus. Our State is a pressure-group State. For example, the problem of strike action will always worry Christians. These are matters of personal ethics and the political theorist may help by pointing out what the function of such action is in a society of democratic institutions. The Church as Church would exercise due care in advising its members in such cases; its duty is to advise, however. Where the Church has the duty to act is in cases where the law allows for certain procedure (as, for example, to African workers to form trade unions), and employer organizations suppress such organizations. In such cases the principles that are involved are clear.

The Church may go further in its indirect participation through its influence on its members. Social organization is not naturalistic; it does not come of itself, the outcome of a kind of physical cause-effect history. A long tradition of historical analysis, dating from Plato, has shown that social institutions are the projection of the embodiment of the ideas or thoughts of man. On occasion it may be necessary to suggest to its members to create some social institution to promote a Christian ethic in that particular sphere, be it the world of the Press, amusement, economics, commerce or high society. This type of action is easily possible in our secular, neutral State. In this connection it will be advisable for the Church, generally, to promote a policy of decentralization of State function to counteract the inevitable centripetal tendency in the modern State which promotes monopoly, and thus the totalitarian outlook. On occasion—but only very occasionally—it may be necessary for the Church to make use of the power of parliamentary initiation which citizen bodies have in this country. The Church is, after all, a pressure group standing for interests, and it may on occasion become necessary to embody these interests in legislation. Such action may, for instance, become necessary in our times of swiftly moving world-populations when any community or country may run the risk of being swamped by an ethic entirely alien to its own dearest convictions.

It will of course be said, and quite rightly, that the Churches have in fact been applying, perhaps spasmodically and haphazardly, this double policy of criticism and indirect participation since the liberal State came into existence. I believe that the contemporary stage of political development demands that the action of the Church along these lines should be self-conscious and part of its set purpose and policy. If the Church is to make its ethic prevail it must understand the conditions in which the ethic has to function. This condition is the contemporary State as we have described it. Our State is humanistic and liberal; it has not yet cut adrift from its historical values. But, firstly, it is no longer an individualistic State; it is a pluralistic State; it governs a community of pressure groups. And, secondly, it is no longer a negative State, although it is neutral. It is an active, organizing and interfering State. It has been made so by contemporary industrial and scientific development and it will remain so. It is the political function of the Church to assert the ethical consciousness and principles which are to direct this interference.

In life there are many things we hold dear which have been made possible and are kept safe by means of our social and political structure. The guarantee of the safety of these values does not depend on the efficiency of State organization. It depends on the ethic which permeates both the principles of State government and the administration of State policy. In a neutral State a Christian ethic can be maintained only by active self-assertion. The alternative to a Christian ethic, under contemporary industrial, scientific and competitive conditions, is an ethic of materialist utility which at the moment takes the form of profit-making. If a realistic Church does not recognize and use the machinery of the present social structure to assert its legitimate interests the State must develop a confessionalism of its own, which will not be Christian, but naturalistic.

The Disunited Church: Why? and How Long?

by

BENEDICTA ROWE

Women's Christian College, Madras

INTRODUCTION

WORK in an inter-denominational College in India brings home forcibly the tension between the fact of the Church Universal and the fact of the Church Divided.

This paper reproduces the substance of three informal talks[1] given to Indian Christian girls who knew little of the Church outside their own particular part, whichever it might be: Anglican, Baptist, Congregational, Lutheran, Presbyterian, Syrian Jacobite, Syrian Mar-Thoma, etc. The Roman Church was not represented among them, and many were accustomed to distinguish between "Christians" and "Roman Catholics." Church history was, to most of them, a phrase entirely devoid of content. But the problem of inter-communion had brought them face to face with the fact of separation and they wanted to find out "what it all meant." The talks had to be extremely elementary: practically no historical knowledge of any kind could be pre-supposed. It is just possible that a somewhat similar situation may have grown up in lands nearer home than India and thus a simple treatment of the "Why" and "When" of Church division may be of use, however difficult the further and vital question, "How long?"

Publication was far from the mind of the writer, and it is only in answer to a definite request that this simple historical statement is given publicity here, and as an essential part of a wider query.

---

[1] In its original form first reproduced in the "Review of the National Christian Council of India," and later, still in its original form, as a pamphlet by the Central Board of Christian Higher Education, Nagpur. Here, somewhat more briefly, it is given after revision, re-shaping, and with some additional material.

One question should be posed, and to some extent answered, as introduction: Why bother at all with the historical background? A satisfying answer involves a treatise on the meaning of history: but the following points may serve to blaze a trail:

(1) The separated parts of the Church assume a wrong character if contemplated *in vacuo*: for we have, then, nothing to which to relate them except the fact of our own religious experience; and seen only in that context our own part of the Church is likely to assume in our minds the appearance of ultimate reality.

(2) Each separated part can be fully appropriated by its own members, and in any true sense appreciated or understood by others, *only* in relation to (*a*) the rest of the Church; (*b*) the actual situation, or context (spiritual *and* socio-politico-economic) in which it developed its separated life: for its separated life is the product of that situation.

(3) Those who made the breaks had, like other men, many concerns besides their churchmanship. To try to isolate their Church life from their other activities is to make the same mistake as to seek to isolate "the economic man."

(4) One necessary element in reunion is the recovery of a sense of proportion, i.e. of *true* proportion; of the function of one part in relation to all others and to the whole.

(5) The Incarnation was an event in time; this means that something happened both *in* history and *to* history. The-Word-made-Flesh (i.e. God-Redeeming-Man-in-Christ) *is*, since the birth of Christ, in history; whether history be considered as the time-process itself or as the comment on that process, it can now never dispossess itself of The-Word-made-Flesh. Thus the Incarnation is both "done" and "a-doing" (both Event and Process). Therefore with regard to the divisions of the Body of Christ:

the genesis of the divisions,
the articulation of a rich Church life in the divisions,
the injury to the life of the whole resulting from the divisions,
the mutual contact of the divisions,

the ultimate healing of the divisions,

the distant centuries, or perhaps millennia, of a re-united Church Universal (if such is to be);

all these are moments, or events, within that Process which is the extension of the Incarnation in the time-process; and, *as such*, claim from us attention to their actual historical contexts. Consider, for example, the immense amount now recovered as to the actual historical context of the life of our Lord, to the very great enrichment and illumination of our faith.

This seems a high-sounding background for a very simple historical outline, but it is only as related to this great background that such an outline can have any value at all; and it was considerations such as these which made it seem worth while to try to salvage for those young members of the Church Universal something of their heritage in history. Furthermore, it is only against such background that any realistic approach to the vital query, How long? can be essayed.

I

I am going to start with something very simple. Where did the Christian Church begin? What was its place of origin?

Palestine: we go back approximately 2,000 years and we find a small new society numbering just a few hundreds, mostly Jews. And gradually this society has spread into every part of the world.

We will begin by looking at the first 300 years. What do we find happening in the Church during those first three centuries after the coming of Christ? The Church[1] was growing. Down the roads and highways radiating out from Palestine, along the coasts, across the seas, to this town and that, the message passed. The new life took root; and men

[1] Strictly speaking, the word "Church" should be kept for the one undivided body of the Faithful, and some other word, such as "communion," "part," "group," should be used for the various divisions; but, for convenience, I have used the word "Church" also for the different parts, though actually to speak of this or that "Church" or of the "Churches" (in the plural) is inexact. There is only one Church, but it is divided by many schisms.

and women were gathered into the new fellowship, were baptized in the name of the Father, the Son, and the Holy Spirit, and, confessing Jesus as Lord, were brought into the Church—became members in the new Society of those whose life was hid with Christ. All these were not simply individual Christians, living separate lives, but first and foremost they were members of the Christian fellowship in whatever place they lived—members of the Christian Church in that place. Thus, not only each individual Christian but each group of Christians became a living cell in the Body of Christ from which fresh life spread. This was the way in which the Church grew. There was no other way.

The Church grew not only in numbers but in strength, developing within itself an organization which preserved unity and a common standard in faith and worship, even though its members were scattered in little isolated groups throughout the length and breadth of the whole Roman Empire and far beyond, and included men and women of every race of that world, and of every variety of social status and background.

Not only the growth of the Church, but the organization of the Church is one of the marvels of human history. It developed an organization at once so flexible and yet so stable that the Roman Government itself began to see that the Christian Church was a living force, perhaps the strongest living power in the Empire.

And so the time came when the Roman Empire began to think of the Christian Church, not as something to be suppressed, but as something to be used—something which might be a valuable source of rejuvenation and unity to the Empire. The Empire itself was beginning to decay, but the Emperor saw that here in the Christian Church was something pulsating with life.

This brings us to a second period. After three centuries had passed since the birth of Christ, the Emperor Constantine, in the year 313, recognized Christianity as a "lawful religion" and, later, gave the Church a privileged position under his own patronage. Had the little Jewish society from Palestine captured the Roman Empire? Or had the Empire captured the Church? Some aspects of the later history of the Church show us beyond doubt that there *were* two sides to that picture.

The decree of Constantine meant the end of persecution and the beginning of prosperity: it also meant the beginning of control and patronage. These things brought loss as well as gain; gaining place and prosperity, the Church lost something of its early purity and fervour. It no longer required courage or even great sincerity to proclaim oneself a Christian: on the contrary, to be a Christian was henceforth simply the normal and respectable thing to be. Already, most Christians were, like ourselves, hereditary Christians whose faith was part of their family heritage and not necessarily rooted in personal conviction. When persecution ceased and Christianity became respectable, there was no longer any external test of the reality of a man's faith: while many unworthy motives might now lead men to profess Christ. Henceforth, therefore, the Church carried a dead weight of nominal Christians.

In course of time, Christianity became the official State religion. This brought another danger. To the Roman Emperors, religion was a department of government. When Christianity became the accepted State religion, the Christian clergy inevitably became to some extent officials as well as pastors. There was danger, too, to the spiritual life of the Church, even in the care with which the Emperor watched over the interests of the Church. He looked upon himself as the patron and protector of the Church, and so when the Church got into difficulties he stepped in.

The most important occasion of such interference by the Emperor was when the Church found itself divided on a matter of doctrine. Thinking men will always ask: "How can these things be?" And one inevitable question for Christians is: "What do you think of Christ? Whose Son is He? What do you mean when you describe Him as both God and Man?" Some thinkers will answer in one way and some in another. This is what happened in the time of Constantine, and the Emperor used his authority to summon a Church Council in order that the Church might arrive at a common mind in regard to the Christian Faith. This was a useful exercise of his authority; but he did not stop there.

After the Council, he issued imperial decrees enforcing the decisions reached as binding on all Christians, and he exiled the man Arius, whose teaching had been rejected, and his followers who still clung to their own opinions. Henceforth, whenever there were disputes in the Church, there was a likelihood of the emperors stepping in, on one side or the other, and this meant that Church questions became involved in statecraft.

Another factor in the life of the Church at this time was the development of local or regional pride and jealousies. There were four great ancient Churches, each pre-eminent in its own area: Antioch (Syria); Alexandria (Egypt); Rome (Western Mediterranean); Constantinople (Eastern Mediterranean). The Church in Jerusalem had originally a pre-eminent position, but it declined in influence after the Romans sacked Jerusalem in A.D. 70.

II

Under Constantine, Constantinople (Ancient Byzantium) became the capital of the Roman Empire, and the Church in Constantinople began to assume particular importance, especially in the eastern half of the Empire: Antioch and Alexandria resented this. To some extent there was an underlying current of national or racial feeling, a Syrian and Egyptian anti-Byzantine feeling. When the Emperor issued edicts enforcing the decisions of the various Church Councils, the Church at Antioch and the Church at Alexandria resisted—they were not going to be dictated to by Constantinople; and, in the end, each broke away from Constantinople, though some people in each continued in communion with Constantinople and formed the Orthodox (i.e. Byzantine) Patriarchates of Antioch and Alexandria which have continued as parts of the Eastern Orthodox Church to the present day: but the great majority of Christians in Syria and Egypt were henceforth members of the separate Syrian and Egyptian Churches and despised their "Orthodox" brethren as "King's men."

These schisms were partly coloured by theological disputes. The Syrian Church was largely Nestorian. Nestorian teaching emphasized the humanity of Christ in such a way as to weaken belief in His full divinity. The Egyptian (or Coptic) Church became Monophysite. Monophysite teaching emphasized the divinity of Christ in such a way as to weaken belief in His actual humanity. General Church Councils which were summoned to consider these teachings refused to accept either as the true teaching of the Church about Christ, for each left out something to which both Christian experience and the New Testament bore witness. But the Syrian Church clung to Nestorian and the Coptic Church to Monophysite teaching. The theological differences could probably have been overcome—as one writer said: "Whereas they differ in word they agree in meaning"—but Antioch and Alexandria would not be dictated to by Constantinople, and national local feeling inflamed the disputes, and so the Syrian and Egyptian Churches clung to their own ways.

Outside the limits of the Roman Empire there were other Christians, especially in Persia. Persia had for centuries been the enemy of Rome. Now that the Roman Emperor had so much say in the Christian Church, the Persian Government began to persecute the Christians in Persia, especially any that had dealings with Constantinople; but when an imperial decree expelled the Nestorians from Syria (which was still a part of the Roman Empire) many Nestorians fled to Persia. Thus a combination of circumstances led to the separation of the Persian Church from the Church of the Roman Empire. This Persian Church, or "Church of the East," to give it its own name, became Nestorian—and is sometimes referred to as the Nestorian Church and sometimes as the East Syrian Church.

The West Syrian Church (i.e. the Church of Antioch), once largely Nestorian, in course of time was influenced by the Egyptian Church and became instead Monophysite. This Church was later known as the Jacobite Church (probably after a certain Jacobus Zanzalus who lived about A.D. 555). To the north were the Christians in Armenia, who also organized themselves as a separate Church and adopted Monophysite teaching; while to the south, in Africa, Abyssinia was evangelized from Egypt and a daughter Church was established there. Thus there grew up, in

60

separation from each other and from the Western Churches, five Asiatic and African Churches: (1) The East Syrian Nestorian Church in Persia, the "Church of the East"; (2) the Church in Armenia; (3) the West Syrian, or Jacobite, Church in Syria, with its centre at Antioch; (4) the Egyptian, or Coptic Church, with its centre at Alexandria; (5) the Abyssinian Coptic Church. Here is the first crop of divisions, the fifth century divisions.

The ancient Eastern Churches, and especially the Nestorian "Church of the East," spread the gospel in Asia. The Nestorians planted their Church in Turkestan, in India, in Central Asia and in China. But dissensions and divisions among themselves, separation from and neglect by the Western Churches, mutual ignorance and jealousy between East and West, stultified their growth; it was Islam and Buddhism, and not the Christian Church, which reaped the harvest in North Africa and Asia.

There is no room here to tell the story of the advance and retreat of Christianity in Africa and Asia during those centuries which we know in Europe as the "Middle Ages"; yet it is a story which needs to be studied, with all its glory and all its shame, in order to see the European Churches in their true perspective.

There came a time when, for long centuries, African and Asiatic Christians were trodden under foot; but, except in China and North India, fragments of all those ancient Eastern Churches, once so great and learned, so enlightened and so vigorous, survive. To-day, all show signs of new life: all had representatives at the Edinburgh World Conference in 1937. Isolation and persecution have driven them in upon themselves, and there is no doubt much in their practices which is backward and superstitious; but the power of renewal is there and the closer contact with the rest of the Christian world which is now beginning will bring fresh inspiration. They, in their turn, have something to give: not only does the story of their survival reveal elements of heroic faith, but in their beautiful liturgies, so jealously guarded, we touch hands with the Church of the early centuries and find elements of Christian thought and devotion which will enrich the whole Church.

It is important to note that the result of schism was a number of regional Churches, each comprising practically the whole Christian population of one area. The same is true of the eleventh-century schism which was to separate Rome and Constantinople. The sixteenth-century schisms in the Western Church, which were to be the outcome of the Reformation, produced, on the contrary, a number of what we might call "confessional" Churches, divided fundamentally, not on a regional, but on a doctrinal basis, though regional feeling played its part. Regional schisms are largely the result of local and communal feeling: to-day we stand on the threshold of closer contact with people all the world over, and this should mean a breaking down of communal barriers; but love for one's own community, like family love, is a valuable and creative element in the common life, and should surely be appropriated by the Church Universal as seasoning to the vaguer emotion of universal fellowship. Churches of the "confessional," rather than the regional, type can emerge only in a society in which individualism has begun fruitfully to assert itself. "Confessional" schisms are perhaps a species of "growing pains," of which the fully-developed body corporate will appropriate the benefit while outgrowing and forgetting the pains.

III

We turn again to the Church within the Roman Empire. Let us look at it in the year A.D. 600, when Augustine, the Roman missionary, had been three years in Britain. By that date the western part of the empire lay in ruins. For centuries Rome had looked across her frontier, the rivers Rhine and Danube, at a restless sea of barbarian tribes, Teutons and Slavs. Now the Teutons had broken into the Empire, and in the west the barbarian tribes settled down in what we know as France and Spain and Italy and Britain. The eastern part of the Empire was still intact and was still ruled from Constantinople by an emperor who was in the direct succession to Constantine.

The unity of the Empire had gone. But the unity of the Church remained; the framework of the Church, both in eastern and western Europe, had survived the shock which had shattered the framework of the Empire. The Church had proved to be the most living thing in the old Roman world, and the clergy set themselves the task of converting the Barbarians to Christ: and so gradually all those who settled down in the old Empire became Christians, and during the following centuries those who were outside the limits of the old Roman Empire were also Christianized. Meanwhile, the people of Eastern Europe, mostly Slavs, were Christianized from Constantinople (Byzantium). Thus there were two great centres of the Church in Europe, Rome and Constantinople.

The evangelization of the Teutons and the Slavs took the form of mass conversions, since for these people, still at a primitive stage, religion was not yet a personal matter: generally speaking, if the King and the Elders accepted Christianity, the whole mass of the people followed suit. The Barbarians had, for the most part, already outgrown their own primitive beliefs and were ready to accept the higher religion of the people whom they conquered. And they were especially ready to learn from the clergy of the Roman Empire, because they wanted to take over all they could of Roman civilization, and by the fifth century you could not separate Roman civilization from Christianity. And so the Church became a great civilizing force, handing on to the Barbarians, not only Christianity, but also some fragments of the culture of the old Roman world, and through the Church a new civilization took shape, the civilization of medieval Europe.

It was a civilization which we might describe as Church-centred, because everything that people did came under the influence of the clergy in some way or other: farming, trade, education, art; even justice, taxation, and government. You couldn't get away from the clergy. They were everywhere, with something to say about everything, and very often with interests and rights and duties of their own in all these matters.

Medieval civilization was Church-centred in another sense. Everybody, man, woman and child, king or beggar, Scot or Italian, all were Church members—whatever else they might be, they all had this in common, they were all members of the same Church. And so, within the framework of the Church, the people of Europe developed into the nations that we know.

The phrase "the framework of the Church" brings us to the subject of the Church organization. It is clear from the New Testament that our Lord's followers formed a new society, a definite group, with certain conditions of membership. But, however much we search the New Testament, we cannot find anything to suggest that our Lord gave any plan for the organization of the new society, except that He left it a group of leaders to whom He had given very special training and teaching. And when we turn to the early years of the young Church we cannot find any clear picture of just how it was organized, so that this is a subject on which men of the utmost learning, piety and devotion differ. But we have clear evidence as to what the arrangement was, at any rate in Asia, by the end of the first century A.D. There is complete evidence that by the turn of the century the Church in Asia was organized under local overseers whose title in Greek has become our "bishop," and everyone is agreed that, before long, this system became universal.

The bishop had a double responsibility: he had to watch over his flock, clergy and laity—he was their shepherd, their father; he also had to act as the link between his flock and the rest of the Church. This system of episcopacy was universal in the Church, certainly from the end of the second century, and has been continued without a break in the Roman Church, in the Churches of Eastern Europe (the Byzantine or "Orthodox" Church and its sister Churches in the Balkans, Russia, etc.), and in all the ancient Eastern Churches already mentioned. In Western Europe it continued as the accepted system until the sixteenth century, and then various groups of Christians abolished episcopacy because they felt that instead of safeguarding the life of the Church it was stifling that life. The rise of these non-episcopal Churches in Western Europe is part of the Protestant Reformation. But during the whole of the Middle Ages the rightness of episcopacy was hardly questioned. It was generally believed that the bishops were the direct successors of the Apostles and that this system had been established by Christ Himself.

At the head of the Western Church stood the Bishop of Rome, the Pope, who was regarded as the direct successor of St. Peter. In the early centuries of the Church the bishops of the four leading cities were given the title of Patriarch (a name taken from the President of the Jewish Sanhedrin). Antioch and Alexandria were cut off from the rest of the Church, first by the fifth-century schisms and then by the Moslem conquest in the seventh and eighth centuries, but Constantinople and Rome remained for many centuries fully united, forming the one undivided Church of what had once been the Roman Empire.

Eastern Christendom looked to Constantinople; Western Christendom looked to Rome. Although fully united, the two parts of the Church developed rather differently and the differences became accentuated through their political separation when, as a result of the Barbarian invasions, Western Europe was lost to the Roman Emperors, who still continued to rule in Constantinople. Rome began to turn its back on Constantinople and to look westward. Quarrels broke out: each was jealous of the claims of the other. The breach between them widened: the two parts of the old Roman Empire were developing on quite different lines; and at last, in 1054, there came a quarrel which has never been healed, as a result of which the Eastern and Western Churches have remained separated from each other, to their great mutual loss, to the present day.

The Eastern Church is known as the Orthodox, or Byzantine, Church and includes sister Churches in the Balkans, in Russia and elsewhere. The Western Church split, in the sixteenth century, into the Roman Church and a number of non-Roman Churches, i.e. Churches which rejected the claims of the Bishop of Rome to be the head of the Church. The Eastern Church is organized as a family of local Churches which are described as "autokephalous," i.e. each has its own head and none is subordinate to another; the Patriarchate of Constantinople has a "primacy of honour" among them, but not any power of control.

The Roman conception of unity is different. From

a comparatively early date, the Bishop of Rome had claimed a primacy over the whole Church. Roman Catholics are taught that Christ gave St. Peter an office of authority over the whole Church; that it is only by recognition of such a central authority that unity can be preserved; that St. Peter was the first Bishop of Rome; and that the Pope, as his successor, inherits his authority. Roman Catholics therefore believe that to break away from the Pope is to break away from St. Peter, and from the society which Christ founded; thus every division in the Church is regarded by Roman Catholics as a desertion from the true Church whose centre is Rome.

This view of the Church developed only gradually. In the early medieval Church the Pope's position was pretty much that of Patriarch of the West, a position giving a "primacy of honour" (like that of Constantinople in the East), but not any right of control. It is perhaps worth noting that in England during the four centuries 669–1050 there were 376 bishops appointed and that the Pope had no share in any of these appointments. But as centuries went on, for many reasons (some greatly to the credit of the Papacy, others equally discreditable), the Pope came to occupy a position of very great authority throughout Western Christendom, until at last he might have been more truly described as Emperor of the Church than as Shepherd of Christ's Flock.

The Church of medieval Europe was to some extent heir to the grandeur and authority of the Roman Empire, and this led to a mistaken idea of authority. Authority in the Church was thought of as much the same kind of thing as authority in the world, as conferring honour and wealth and power; positions in the Church often brought great power and wealth and dignity, and bishops were regarded as princes, so that the whole tone of the clergy tended to be infected with worldliness, and all the more because the medieval Church was so completely entangled in medieval society.

I spoke of the Church as a great civilizing force during the centuries after the fall of Rome, and I described medieval civilization as "Church-centred." I want to say a little more about this. Before Constantine there was a clear line between

66

Christians and the rest of society. To be a Christian might be dangerous. The Christians knew themselves to be a body set apart. After Constantine, Christianity became the accepted religion of the Empire and the Christian Church gradually absorbed the bulk of the population. Then came the fall of the Empire and the conversion of the Barbarians, and a new Europe arose. In medieval Europe everyone was a Christian as a matter of course from infancy. This expansion of the Church to cover the whole population meant: (*a*) that all had the way of Christ open to them from childhood, *but* (*b*) that many were regarded as Christians and as full members of the Church for whom religion never became a personal reality at all. The idea of the Church received a tremendous extension, but it was stretched beyond reality. The medieval world was a Christian world in one sense, but only a few people in it were truly converted Christians, truly surrendered to Christ. As a result, the whole standard of Christian faith and practice was in danger. Perhaps some such identification with the world was necessary for the Church, in order that the Church should realize its responsibility towards the world and for "the redemption of the political and social order." The early Church prayed for itself and its members and for the conversion of all men, but it did not, I think, accept responsibility before God for the regeneration of the whole of human society. This sense, so marked in modern Christianity, comes to us partly as a result of those long centuries in which the Western Church identified itself with the total population of its world. But the dangers were very great. The society whose life is hid with Christ had become identified with the whole population of Western Europe long before the people had emerged from semi-barbarism or were really converted, and the teaching of the Church gathered all sorts of superstitions; the life of the Church was marred by abuses and superstitious practices, whilst the officers of the divine society, who were to have been the servants of their fellows, became a great and powerful corporation.

Yet if any are tempted to dwell on the faults of the medieval Church, let them remember that the book which many people choose to keep beside the Bible is a book written by a medieval priest, a monk of the later Middle Ages, "The Imitation of Christ," by Thomas à Kempis, and this will remind them that the Medieval Church was still in very truth the Temple of the Holy Spirit.

Let us turn also to some of the hymns that we sing because we recognize in them a simple devotion to Christ which we wish might be ours:

> O Jesus, King most wonderful,
>
> .　　.　　.　　.　　.
>
> Thee may our tongues for ever bless,
> Thee may we love alone,
> And ever in our lives express
> The image of Thine own.

This comes to us from another medieval monk, St. Bernard. And there is a prayer that we all love to use:

> May we know Thee more clearly,
> Love Thee more dearly,
> Follow Thee more nearly.

This is the prayer of one of the medieval bishops, Richard, Bishop of Chichester. Not all people realize how deep is our debt to the "evangelical" piety of the Middle Ages. But the best witness to the spiritual power of the medieval Church is the Christian heritage of Western Europe. All those to whom Christianity has come by way of Western Europe are the spiritual children of the medieval Church.

IV

We come now to the next great Age of Divisions, the sixteenth century, the time when the visible unity of the Western Church was at last broken. The later fifteenth century and early sixteenth century was a time when there was great corruption in some parts of the Church, notably in the Papacy, which was by then very nearly all-powerful in the Western Church. It was a time also when the spirit of reform and change was stirring everywhere in Western Europe. There were many movements of reform in different parts of the Church during the fifteenth century. It was a time also of very great intellectual activity, the time of the Renaissance;

a time in which there was a great increase in education, especially among the trading classes; and it was the period which saw the invention of printing. One result was that Bibles, which had hitherto, like other books, been available only in very expensive hand-written copies, became now plentiful and fairly cheap: so that the Bible became much more readily accessible just at a time when many more people were able to read. Great scholars devoted themselves to studying the Bible and lecturing on it. For more than a century there had been a reform movement at work in the Church, and, linked with it, a movement for checking the power of the Pope and for reforming the Papacy itself; but the whole Church system had become so rigid and so mixed up with vested interests that the reformers had not made much headway. What was needed was not a reform movement, but a revolution. And now, through the greater knowledge of the Bible, which was spreading, it was as though God had called His Church back to the hills of Galilee. This revival of Bible-study had the effect of a great purifying wind blowing through the Church, fanning the flame of reform, and the flame of revolt against the corrupted Papacy, into a great blaze.

The first man who successfully defied the Papal authority and broke away from the medieval Church was the German monk, Martin Luther. Once the Lutheran movement was fairly launched, other revolts followed, breaking out spontaneously as the spirit of reform and of opposition to Rome carved fresh channels for itself, and as the temperament and genius of different leaders shaped its course. The most important of such leaders after Luther was Calvin. From the work and teaching of Calvin there developed Calvinist Churches in Switzerland, Holland, Scotland, parts of France, and among some groups in England. Other leaders carried out other types of Reformation and built up other Churches.

In all this there were certain ideas and influences which coloured the reform movement wherever it showed itself. I will mention two.

1. People were becoming very conscious of the value of national organization. A compact unit, with a strong ruler at the head of it who would keep things peaceful and orderly

inside the country and do the best he could for his own country in his dealings with the outside world: this seemed the ideal organization for any people; the old medieval conception of Christendom as one unit was gone (it had never been a political reality), and Europe was shaping itself into the self-contained, self-regardant nation-states of the modern world. To some extent the spirit of reform was captured by the spirit of the nation-state and the Church was trimmed and shaped to fit into this framework.

2. At the same time, people were becoming very conscious of the marvellous powers of the human mind and will. It was the age of discovery and of scientific inventions. And it was an age in which there was a growing appreciation of the value of the individual man and woman.

Now, the first feeling (that of the importance of the nation as a unit) naturally made people think that the government had both the right and the duty of settling everything, including religion, within the country.

The second feeling (that of the value of the individual mind and will) would lead at least some people to assert their own opinions and their own wills both in politics and in religion, and this might bring them into conflict and trouble with the government. Both forces played their part in shaping the course of the Reformation.

And everywhere secular and selfish motives were at work to side-track and distort the purely spiritual impulse of a return to the New Testament and a purification of Church life and worship. This should not surprise us when we remember how the disciples themselves disputed, in the very presence of Christ, as to who should be greatest; when we think of what St. Paul's letters show us about the lives of the Corinthian Christians; and when we think of ourselves and of how often unworthy motives get mixed up with what we would like to think are our deepest spiritual impulses— national, communal and class pride and jealousies; personal affections and antipathies; self-interest and self-assertion; economic advantages in one form or another; considerations of taste and temperament. It is not surprising that the course of the Reformation was coloured by political and economic influences, and that everywhere political and religious quarrels combined to produce civil wars: wars which, however much they might be fought in the name of religion, were, truth to tell, largely concerned with secular or political ambitions. But all this must not obscure for us the truth that the reformation movement itself, the separatist Churches which resulted from it, and the "Counter-Reformation" which purified the Papacy and the Roman Church, are a fresh manifestation of the life hidden in the heart of the Christian community.

V

The medieval Church had been the Church of the whole of western Europe, but in the sixteenth century Church life began to flow in national channels and it seemed as though there might be a separate Church for each nation. It was a generally accepted principle that the government of a country should recognize one form of Church and that the subjects of that government should be expected to conform to the recognized Church. Thus in many countries the Roman Church was the only recognized Church; whilst in those countries which broke with Rome, generally speaking, one or other of the non-Roman Churches was recognized as the State Church. In some countries there is still a recognized "State" Church, e.g. in Spain and Eire the Roman Church is the officially recognized State Church; in Scotland, the Presbyterian Church is the Church of Scotland; in Sweden and Prussia, the Lutheran is the State Church—in Prussia, at any rate, until recently; in England, the non-Roman Episcopalian—or, as it is commonly called, the Anglican—Church is the Church of England.

But it is worth noticing that the relationship between these national Churches and the State is the result, in each case, of particular historical circumstances, and not the logical outcome of their theological doctrines, e.g. the Calvinist Church in Scotland became the national Church of Scotland, yet in France and in England Calvinist Churches exist which are not the national Churches. The Lutheran Church became the national Church in Prussia, but Lutheran Churches in the South German states are not the national

Churches. The non-Roman Episcopalian Anglican Church became the national Church in England, yet the Episcopalian Churches in America and in Scotland are not national Churches but "Free" Churches.

Thus, a study of the national Churches shows that, even at a time when the authority of the national government was triumphing everywhere, the life of the Christian Church could not be kept simply in national channels: it broke through the national mould everywhere. This is seen in all its force in the story of the "Free Churches," i.e. those Churches which have no connection with the State and which have had to maintain their right to exist in the face of State opposition.

Once the unity of the Western Church was broken, in all countries groups of people arose who, finding in the Bible or in their own spiritual experience some truth which they felt to be vital to spiritual life and which they prized above everything else, gathered together and tried either to get their ideas accepted for the whole nation, or, if this proved impossible, insisted on organizing themselves as a group apart from the national Church, and demanded freedom to set up whatever form of Church organization appealed to them and the right to worship as their conscience directed. And everywhere, sooner or later, the national Church, whatever it might be, took steps together with the national government to suppress such groups and force them back into uniformity; and so such groups fought the battle for freedom of thought, freedom of speech and freedom of worship. Such were the Baptists, the Congregationalists, the Quakers, the Unitarians, and others. Many of the American states owe their origin to groups of people who left their homes in Europe and in England and began life afresh in America in order that they might be free to worship God in the way that they thought right. Even these people did not all, at first, resist the temptation to force their views on others; and in some of the New England states of America the dominant Church, whatever it was, tried to suppress other sects of which it disapproved. But, generally speaking, America was from the first the home of religious liberty, and, as a result, of religious experiment.

A special word is necessary about the development of the Anglican Church at the time of the Reformation. The principle underlying the Anglican Reformation was to repudiate the Papal authority as a usurped authority, a perversion of episcopacy, but at the same time definitely to preserve all that was felt to be good in the medieval heritage, i.e. all that was believed to be in conformity with the plain teaching of the New Testament and with the teaching of the leaders of the "undivided Church"—the expressions of faith, for instance, contained in the Apostles' and the Nicene Creeds which had been accepted in the Church before even the fifth-century schisms took place.

The Anglican Church at the time of the Reformation was influenced by Lutheranism, and still more at one time by Calvinism, but it deliberately refused to be either Lutheran or Calvinist, believing that neither was fully true to the witness of the New Testament or to the faith of the early Church. The Anglican reformers rejected the thought of founding a "new" society or of finding new channels in which Church life might flow. They took very special care to preserve continuity with the medieval Church, and, through the medieval Church, with the early Church, believing that the channel through which Church life should flow had been marked out by Christ and by the Holy Spirit acting through the early disciples, and that what was needed was not a change, but a cleansing of the old channel. The Anglican Church stood by the belief that the structure of the Church, the organization of its life throughout the centuries up till that very moment, through the triple ministry of deacon, priest and bishop, was not accidental, but that this was the external form through which the life of the Church, and, above all, its unity, expressed itself— not something added, but something which grew out of the very nature of the Church as created by the Gospel and the fact of Christ. To the Anglicans, as to the Roman Catholics, the structure of the Church appeared as something vitally relevant to the function of the Church; the bishops, in direct succession from the Apostles, performing in the Church all down the ages the functions of the apostolate as founded by Christ in the early Church, guarding the faith and unity of the whole body, and standing as the necessary links by which the passing centuries were related to each other and each part related to the whole. This part of the teaching of the medieval and early Church the Anglican reformers were not prepared to give up, believing that it was indeed the message of the New Testament, and that no one part of the Church, no particular group of Christians, had the right on their own authority to reject it. Thus the Anglican Church preserved episcopacy and took special pains to preserve the "Apostolic Succession" of its bishops.

Other reformed Churches thought that this view of episcopacy was not proved to be the message of the earliest years or of the New Testament; and in setting up, as they did, new types of ministries, without seeking ordination from the bishops, they felt that they were drawing upon a Christian experience as significant as the development of episcopacy itself—the indwelling of any group of believers by the Holy Spirit, and the "priesthood" of every true believer (Matt. xviii. 20: "Where two or three . . ."; 1 Peter ii. 9: "ye are . . . a royal priesthood . . ."). These were truths which the medieval Church had forgotten, or at any rate had failed to emphasize, and which the Anglican and other Episcopalian Churches saw less clearly than the Free Churches. The Episcopalian Churches, on the other hand, realized more clearly than the separated Churches the significance of the "wholeness" of the Church as one body, and the need for the separate groups and congregations and the individual believers to "lose" their separate life in the common life. Generally speaking, where episcopacy has been abandoned there has been no check to the process of division; on the other hand, episcopacy has sometimes tended to stifle the life of the Church, rather than to safeguard it.

One split occurred in the Anglican Church when in the eighteenth century its spiritual life was at a low ebb, and a revivalist movement inspired by John Wesley was driven into revolt by the opposition and indifference of the Church authorities. Driven to desperation, Wesley took the step of establishing a separated ministry, which was not recognized by the Church. This was the origin of the Methodist Church.

At the world conferences on "Faith and Order," there has been unanimous agreement that the chief need in all the Christian bodies to-day is to come to a better understanding of the nature of the Church. Any attempt to meet the question: How long must disunity remain? is presumptuous without such understanding. Any attempt to understand the nature of the Church and the significance of the present divisions must go back to the Church in the New Testament as a starting point.

"Jesus Christ did not come into a religious vacuum. He was born into a community that believed itself to be the People of God."[1] The word which He used for the society which He founded was the word translated in the Greek as *ecclesia*, which we render as "Church." Its meaning for our Lord and His disciples was determined by its use in the *Septuagint* for the phrase "the congregation of Israel." In effect, our Lord said to St. Peter, after his confession of faith: "On this rock I will found my Israel." His disciples deliberately chose this word *ecclesia* ("the congregation of Israel," or of the *new* Israel) to describe the new society of those who professed Jesus as Lord and were baptized into His company.

This is the Church viewed in its corporate capacity. The conception of the Church as a great society, a divinely inspired unity, is not something added to the Gospel by men because it is convenient: it lies at the very heart of the Gospel itself. Consider our Lord's application to Himself and His followers of the established Old Testament metaphor for God and His people—the Shepherd and His flock. More significant still is the application to Himself and His followers of the Old Testament metaphor of the Vine: He *is* the Vine, and His followers the branches. Their life flows from Him; the branches have no life in separation. Christ did not say: "I am the root of the vine," or "the stem of the vine"; but "I *am* the vine"—the very vine itself in its totality. The Christian community is presented as an organic unity.

[1] The Bishop of Dornakal (a Pamphlet on "The Ecclesia of Christ").

Any society, even a divine society, of men and women living in the world presupposes some degree of organization, however slight. Some act of admission, some general principles of action through which the purpose of the society is achieved, some recognized authority, however chosen, which can act on behalf of the members and represent the society to the outside world and to itself. The Book of Acts and the Epistles of St. Paul show us the young society evolving for itself the organization through which the new life could express itself, evolving its organization—by prayer, through the guidance of the Holy Spirit, and with certain things already given by its Lord—baptism, the Supper of the Lord, the Apostles, i.e. the sacraments and the ministry. The outline of the new organization is clearly traced for us in Acts and Epistles. It consisted in common prayer, common charity, common worship (in the Temple and in the Breaking of Bread), common faith, and a recognized rite of initiation—namely, baptism and the laying on of hands.

How did the members know what they believed? By "the Apostles' teaching." How did they preserve their unity? By a recognized organization and through recognized leaders. All this flowed from the experience of the new life in Christ which the first disciples held in trust for mankind. "Through the death and Resurrection of Jesus Christ the people of God had passed through death into newness of life." The Christian Faith is not the result of private speculation, but something "given" to man. The Church is the steward of the mysteries of Christ. The Christian experience is something which must be shared to be fully known and must find ways of corporate expression, since Christ Himself called men and women, not into an isolated relationship with Himself, but into a fellowship through which Israel, the servant of God, should be re-born for the salvation of the human race. You cannot live the full Christian life in deliberate isolation from the Christian society: you can live a very beautiful and in some ways almost a Christ-like life in deliberate isolation or separation from the Christian society, *but* it is something less than the life which Christ left to His followers and to which He calls them.

But this is not the whole secret of the Church: there is a double thread in the New Testament Church. It is true that the full Christian life cannot be lived in deliberate isolation from the Christian society: yet it is equally true that the secret of the Christian life lies in the isolation of the soul before God; the individual soul face to face with Christ. Consider how much of Christ's teaching turns upon the need for a personal decision. Christ's claim is a claim on the whole personality and therefore it can be met only by an individual and personal response. The relationship of man to God is a relationship of love, and love must be a personal act. The Christian Faith centres in the supreme significance of the individual soul.

So, from the Gospel comes the sense of the significance of the Church as a divinely ordered community whose life is nourished from roots reaching far back into history— a community rooted in particular events in the history of a particular people, the Jews, which through being used by God has become of profound significance for the whole human race. But equally from the Gospel comes the sense of the significance of the Church as the means by which the individual soul appropriates the gift of life in Christ.

So we have the double *foci* of the Christian life—the Church and the individual brought into the Church. The Church is prior to the individual Christian: the individual is brought into the Church. This is true to the facts: thus it was and is. Christ constituted a group and calls souls into it. (Cf. St. Paul in 1 Cor. xii. 12, where he uses "Christ" where one would expect the word "Church"—"so also is the Christ," i.e. Christ = Church.) But the Church exists for the sake of the individual. This also is true. Behind that original group in the Upper Room lay their several individual acts of choice: each chose Christ for himself; a personal choice which no one else could make for him. But behind even their choice lay His call, His call to Himself, into the true vine which is Himself, His call to union with Himself, and in and through them His call to others.

It is interesting to find in the Student Christian Movement "Christian Year Book" (p. 58) the Roman Catholic Church, the

77

Church which most clearly emphasizes the corporate aspect of Church life, speaking of itself as follows: "The innermost secret of its existence consists in the acceptance of Christ by the individual Catholic and the conversion by which he gives himself, whole mind and spirit and strength, to Christ." Nothing could show more clearly the essential one-ness of the faith held by Roman and Protestant alike. There is in reality no separation between the corporate life of the Church and the individual life in Christ; life flowing forth from the source to return to the source.

In our divided Church there is always a tendency for different parts of the Church to emphasize one aspect of the Christian life and neglect the other, to the great detriment of our own spiritual life and great loss of power. We have seen the significance of the structure of the Church, but we cannot find in the New Testament clear evidence as to the original form of Church organization: some scholars think it differed in different parts. We find evidence in the earliest period of an authority like that of a bishop exercised by St. Paul, with the title of Apostle, and reference to bishops who seem to derive authority from the Apostles, and also evidence of groups of local leaders similar to the modern Presbyterian elders; evidence also of individual local congregations. We cannot settle the historical problem, nor would it help us if we could; the life of the Church cannot be determined by antiquarianism. The sixteenth-century reformers perhaps made a mistake in trying to "get back" to the organization of the primitive Church, ignoring the life of the Church during the fifteen intervening centuries; you cannot get back in that way by study and guesswork to a condition of things which has passed away. The result was the setting up of new ministries and new confessions, bearing valuable witness indeed to neglected aspects of the Christian faith and experience, but inevitably overlooking others equally important. To accept these ministries and confessions means accepting the principle of division, for on this basis where can division end? Here arises the question: How long? It is this situation which has to be faced and thought out.

Behind the unity of the Church there must always be the

indwelling presence of the Holy Spirit within each group of believers and within the individual soul—what we might term the prophetic element in spiritual life; and though the separated Churches seem to betray the cause of unity their fruits are clearly the fruits of the Spirit. A united Church must safeguard the prophetic element in the Christian experience.

Yet there still remains the need to safeguard the "given" element—the fact of Christ. The risks to the faith in an isolated group are seen in St. Paul's letters to the Corinthians and the Colossians, and in Eph. iv. 14. The Faith must be true to the common Christian experience; the local part must be related to the whole. The celebration of the "Lord's Supper" must aim at being according to the intention of the Lord, and that intention included the visible unity of His followers sharing in a common act; and we must face the question whether it can be right to claim to perform that sacred act through ministries appointed without reference to the rest of the Church.

The result of the claim to autonomy on the part of the local congregation, and of the claim to ordain a ministry without reference to the rest of the Church, has been endless division. The determination to make the Bible the sole standard of belief means an open door to every variety of private interpretation and individual doctrinal standard. The perversity and foolishness of the human mind is almost endless and such an approach to the revelation in Christ seems contrary to the New Testament evidence. St. Paul recalls the Corinthians to the teaching that they had received from him, and emphasizes his right to claim the authority of an Apostle. The Christian Society, he declares, is built upon "the foundation of the Apostles and prophets" (Eph. ii. 20). Both the apostolic succession and the prophetic succession seem realities not to be ignored in the life of the Church, realities which complete each other.[1]

Some schisms have certainly been purely factious and the result of pride or self-interest; but, generally speaking, no separated group could have survived, much less grown and shown forth the fruits of the Spirit, unless men had found

[1] *Cf.* E. Underhill, "Worship" (Nisbet, 1936), pp. 231–7.

through it a true means of communion with Christ. Thus, in a sense, every sect and separated Church bears witness to the unquenchable life of the Spirit in the hearts of believers.

The answer to the question: How long? now lies, under God, with all who can in any way help the Church to move towards comprehensiveness, by seeking to find in other parts of the Church, not only those aspects of truth which are obscured in their own and are the necessary complement of those to which their own bears witness, but also to realize and comprehend those very truths for which their own part stands. It may very well be that these are actually represented elsewhere, though represented differently. They may have been recovered, or have received fresh expression, since our spiritual fathers took their stand or made their protest, and the protest may no longer be necessary.

Religion is, to a very large extent, an expression of group life, and there is always danger that it may become *only* that—"our way of acknowledging the existence of God," with the emphasis on *us* and *our*—valued as giving a sanction to traditional customs. The fact that the religion of a group or a country is *called* Christian and poured into the Christian mould is no safeguard. There is a need for it constantly to be brought back to the source of all life, as the Roman Catholic Statement in the "Year Book" puts it: "to the act by which the individual gives himself to Christ."

All the major breakings away from a parent Church have originated because the Church as it existed was to some extent stifling this life: they have all come about because this life refuses to be stifled; so, even in the divisions of the Church, the Spirit bears witness to Himself, even though the divisions may also witness to human weakness and sin, human pride and impatience. But though the need to protest or to witness to some neglected aspect of the truth may have inspired the original generation, it may not at all be the reason why the split continues; there is no safeguard for a protesting Church any more than for a conservative Church that it may not become simply a comfortable shelter for the pride and selfishness of its members. There is for all a continual need for a renewing of the Spirit, and fundamental condition for this is humility and charity.

"Love is not puffed up, setteth not by itself, rejoiceth not in evil." We should apply this to our attitude to other Churches, especially to those most different from our own and most difficult for us to understand. If we approach our divisions in this spirit we shall find ourselves led into united prayer for the restoration of unity. Perhaps the model for such prayer might be some words from a recent pamphlet[1] on the problem of reunion by Fr. W. B. O'Brien, of the Society of St. John the Evangelist: "Our desire is towards Him and His purpose; we do not ask that our views shall prevail . . . but that His will may prevail over us *all*. . . . We do not want Him to give Protestants a victory over Catholics or Catholics a victory over Protestants, but we do wish our Lord to triumph gloriously over all our prejudices, blindnesses, and self-will. Such a prayer . . . would transform us inwardly before we were united outwardly. As *we* were changed much that is now impossible would become not only possible but inevitable. . . . He (the Holy Spirit) does not need to destroy His work in order to fulfil it."

[1] "Christian Unity: the Problem for Anglicans" (The Pax House).

The Predicament of the Church To-Day

by

EMIL BRUNNER

University of Zurich

THE shattering events of these present days and their dark forebodings for the future oblige the Church to give special thought to its own condition and basically to review both its strength and its deficiencies. We are experiencing in the politico-military area the tragic consequences of a certain *laissez faire* in citizenship, an inability to rise to the necessary special exertions, or even to a realistic appraisal of the situation in the face of a threatening danger. Who would contend that we are not confronted in the Church with something analogous? Who would say that all in the Church is well?

We do not desire to paint the devil on the wall; but are we armed against events like those we have seen during the last two decades in great "Christian" countries where the functions of the Church have been either destroyed or greatly compromised through political revolutions, without the Church as a whole even making an effort to offer serious resistance? Is it out of keeping with the times of to-day to cry: Church, awake; act, as long as there is day, for the night is coming when one can act no longer?

THE PLIGHT OF THE CHURCH

The most obvious problem is the widespread decrease of participation in Church life. Statistically, this is not to be observed in an especially frightening degree. The greater part of the population of German Reformed Switzerland, for example, continues to hold to the national Church. The somewhat disquieting confessional missionary activity of the Roman Church in Reformed Zurich can be explained, if one is optimistically inclined, on the grounds of population movement; the relatively insignificant decline in Church membership and the continuing small percentage of persons without any confessional affiliation *could* be regarded as evidence that the Church life of our people is still intact. Moreover, the number of unbaptized, particularly in country areas, is still very small in comparison with the baptized. We get quite another picture, however, when we examine the relative number of those who participate with regularity in the life of the Church, in the Sunday and weekday services, in Communion, in Bible classes or in practical Church activities. When we remind ourselves that in certain urban communities, both middle-class and so-called workers' sections, the population has doubled, trebled and even quadrupled in the last fifty years, while the Sunday church attendance has only barely maintained itself, or that in both urban and rural communities the number of people attending church is often only 5 per cent. of the population, then the language of statistics suddenly acquires another significance.

The question as to how actively the young people, the workers and the leading figures in political, commercial and cultural circles participate in the life of the Church leads to a similar conclusion. How large is the number of our active politicians, businessmen, high-school and college teachers who show themselves at all interested in the Church as an appreciable factor in determining their life outlook? Although it is only in exceptional cases that one can speak of outright opposition to the Church, one cannot escape the fact that in all levels of the population there is fearfully little acquaintance between the Church and the people. We are naturally aware that visible participation in the life of the Church is far from being a proof of one's Christianity, and similarly that lack of participation is not necessarily a sign of denial of the faith; but we also know that a vital Christendom cannot exist in the long run without a vital congregational expression, and that lack of interest in the life of the Church is itself a sign of an impoverished Christianity.

But the widespread decline in active membership, which cannot be denied, is not necessarily a bad sign in itself. On the contrary, it could very well happen that it is precisely a Church filled with the spirit of God that would become a decided minority; the minority character of a Church can be a sign of its spiritual power rather than of its spiritual weakness. The Church has never been promised that, wherever it had opportunity to exercise its influence over a long period of time, it would gradually embrace the entire people. The Constantinian–Theodosian identification of State Church and Church people which dominated the entire Middle Ages, the Reformation and post-Reformation period and which began to totter only after the Enlightenment and the French Revolution, was possible only as a result of a terrific secularization of the Church, a lowering of demands upon the individual to certain external forms compatible with what could be accomplished through State compulsion. A realization of the widespread falling off in active Church life can only have a meaning, if related, therefore, to a corresponding *reduction in intensity* characterizing evangelical life in "Church circles."

To be sure, this second factor is less easy to determine than the first; our conclusions here must be more cautiously formulated if they are to be free from the charge of arbitrariness and arrogance. But in this area, too, there are actualities which cannot be interpreted by any competent observers except as evidence of *reduced intensity*.

The following facts stand out:

(*a*) The Church makes very small demands on its members, and its members do not permit appreciable demands to be made upon them. Neither in the matter of confessional teachings nor in the matter of general Church-Christian upbringing would the "Church people" permit themselves to be controlled by definite standards or even to be measured by such. The great majority of them would immediately protest most violently. Theoretically, the Christian piety which the Church demands of its members may be according to the New Testament, but in practice there prevails a very superficial Christianity, both in teaching and in living. One can scarcely distinguish the difference between those "of" and those "not of" the Church, either in essential faith or in works.

(*b*) Such practices of the Christian life as regularity in prayer, in attendance at services of worship, in family devotions, in Bible reading, have progressively deteriorated even among the small minority which one might describe as Church-related. This, of course, is a fact which cannot be statistically determined, but the judgment is fully grounded in many observations which are symptomatic. One may evaluate the actual extent of this deficiency either optimistically or pessimistically, but no one who knows the life of our people can deny that it is great.

(c) It is only in relatively exceptional cases that one can speak of a life of Christian fellowship, especially in the cities. Whereas people in rural areas at least know one another and display a certain neighbourly sense of mutual responsibility, particularly in circumstances of distress, the members of the city congregation are for the most part strange to one another and show little disposition to become acquainted. And why should they? They have their own friends and associates, with whom they carry on their community and social existence. Even the awareness of what a truly Christian fellowship would be, is completely foreign to most of them. Thus, the Sunday worship service and the Lord's Supper can meagrely be understood as nothing but a personal matter, never rightly as a community experience.

(d) Some acquaintance with Holy Scripture, and even of the most elementary Christian teachings, which at one time was taken for granted as the possession of even those who knew very little of the Bible itself, is disturbingly poor; and naturally a genuine understanding of what these teachings actually mean for the life of the Christian is even rarer. Similarly, the fundamentals of genuinely Christian living are unfamiliar, and there is distressingly little apprehension of the demands of God upon the individual in the varied circumstances of his daily life.

(e) A consciousness of responsibility on the part of the individual to the Church is seldom to be found, and it follows that readiness and initiative for participation in the work of the Church are extremely rare. All manner of other activities take precedence and are brought forward as the reason why one "could not possibly find the time."

(f) Thus it is not to be wondered at that the Church, as a community of the faithful, exerts small determining influence on the life of the people as a whole. People are too often astonished to discover that at least the Romans do expect demands to be made upon them as members of the Church, and that many of them go to great pains to be faithful churchmen.

(g) On the basis of many pastors' experiences it can be quite reliably concluded that very few of the people, including those active in Churches, know anything whatever of the meaning of "the prayer life," "wrestling for salvation," "the experience of the power of Christ and the Holy Spirit in my own life," "walking in the paths of God," or anything else which could be regarded as a definite Christian experience, even when one bears in mind that such experience can exist without any Biblical stimulus whatever.

(h) It is thus understandable that the Church and the Christian life arouse neither admiration nor annoyance, neither desire nor repugnance, but simply are disregarded. Young people in particular are little attracted by the Church, as they are bound to have the feeling that the Christian life is empty convention, that nothing worth mentioning ever happens within the Christian group as such, and that the Church will never make real demands or call a person to high stakes. Their appraisal might well be: the Church seeks to enlist us, but it offers us nothing and demands of us nothing. This may be the exaggeration of youth, but it is not without a large measure of truth. When we consider the eras in the life of the Church when it was most dangerous or most glorious to be a Christian, when the teaching of the Church moved the best minds more than anything else, when the claims of the Church attracted precisely the most courageous, when the standards of the Church were valid and thoroughly recognized even when they were not obeyed—when we remember these things we can measure the depth of the "intensive deficiency" in the Church of our day.

This is not to say that nothing of Christian faith and life still prevails in our Church. On the contrary, experience teaches us that there are many Christians whose belief and whose zeal for Christ are deeply earnest, who genuinely live their faith in prayer and obedience, in intercession and active love.

Nor have conditions especially deteriorated just recently. On the contrary, there exist many gratifying evidences of growth and strengthening in the life of the Church, which can be points of departure for a new awakening. And the demand for the true Church, for solid spiritual food, for the ministry to souls, for fellowship, for definite guidance in practical life is great. This brings us to a second question which leads us deeper.

THE CAUSES OF OUR PRESENT PLIGHT

What are the causes?

We shall necessarily confine ourselves to those causes which lie within the Church itself or for whose consequences the Church is primarily responsible.

1. There is no doubt that the most important is what one might call the *disintegration of the substance of the Church*. In recent centuries the Church has lost increasingly the consciousness of what the Church is and what the Church is for. We can observe this best, though not at all exclusively, in the secularization of theology. The congregation suffers increasingly from spiritual undernourishment and from substitutionary nourishment. What has often been offered has not been that which builds, sustains and increases the Church—the Word of Life. The Gospel is either presented in a lifeless manner that bore no witness, in a manner that was not begotten of a living faith and could not beget a faith, or handed forth as the wisdom of men, idealism, moralism, instead of the Word of God, stones instead of bread.

2. The Reformed National Church, growing out from the national Church of the time of Constantine, has not become aware of the change in its situation and task as a result of the collapse of confessional coercion by the State. For more than a thousand years the Church of coercion prevailed in Europe; membership in the Church through baptism and a certain minimum of Church practices was required and forced for purposes of the State, with the result that there developed an identity of the State folk and the Church folk through a process of naturalization. This condition continued also in the great Churches of the Reformation until the

87

French Revolution. The entire Church organization as well as all Church activity were built on this foundation of a State-created Church. The Church was not allowed to recruit and did not want to evangelize; it rested on the fiction that all the members of the nation were baptized Christians and it could make the pretence that everyone could at least hear its Word because everyone was obliged to hear it. This ended externally with the French Revolution. With the Enlightenment and the awakening of modern humanism the believing Christian community cut itself loose from the world in an inner sense. The situation became somewhat similar to what it had been before Constantine. But the Church did not understand this turning of the road, and accordingly retained its Constantinian heritage in organization and manner of work. It continued to concern itself with the maintenance of the organization rather than with a mission, with the advancement of those who were already Christian in faith rather than with the creation of faith. In organizational structure, in preaching, teaching and pastoral ministry, the orientation was toward the existing congregation and not toward *missionary expansion*. In this regard much of the Church of the past two hundred years has been asleep.

3. The Church has digested no better the tremendous *social upheavals* which have sprung from technical-commercial revolution. The Church of the Middle Ages, the Reformation and the period following the Reformation could reckon with the family, the solidarity of the clan and the clearly defined community as the natural basis for the proclamation of the faith and the building of the congregation. Modern society, however, is largely atomized and disorganized into an unorganic concentration of human beings by machines and mass production and by the liberty of movement of the population. The complete unacquaintance of great masses of people with Christian *mores* has a contagious influence also on those who are closer to the Church and in this way threatens the sense of fraternity from within. The large city rolls the atomized human masses unorganically together. Clubs and social groupings for special purposes replace natural groupings with artificial ones. Yet the Church has scarcely taken notice of this terrific change, or at

least has done nothing practical to meet it. Instead of concentrating on fellowship and cell-groups all the more, it has entirely neglected this function which was so central in apostolic Christianity, because the Church of the intervening centuries, which worked under such completely different presuppositions, offers no pattern! The Church, which according to the teaching and example of the New Testament above all else is a fellowship, has itself been atomized and has concealed from itself the evil of this condition by evoking the vision of an invisible community of the faithful!

4. The Church of the Reformation was orientated in its functional structure around the fact that the minister of the congregation was the natural leader and that the Sunday sermon—as well as the weekday sermon—stood alongside the Bible as practically the only spiritual nourishment of the people. To-day it is scarcely true that the officers of the Church belong to the leading circles of the community; quite different spiritual elements have assumed the leadership; the school, the high school and university, technicians, newspapers, writers and artists. The sermon must stand up against powerful competition in the forms of a voluminous offering of knowledge, culture, entertainment and pleasure. Whereas the word of the Church was formerly almost the only significant public word, to-day it is disappearing under the plethora of what is spoken, printed, seen in the cinema and heard on the radio. In consequence of this condition, the Church should have made numerous and energetic adjustments in the manner of its work. But the Church has done as good as nothing. It continues to be orientated entirely towards the minister and his weekly sermon, and shows great surprise when this preoccupation no longer commands the former attention.

5. The life of the people in earlier centuries was confined by custom and natural necessities in definite moulds; life was comparatively simple. Modern civilization with rushing tempo, its entanglements and its incomprehensibility, with its continuous shoving about of human beings and its changes of conditions, constantly confronts people with new situations and new problems which previously were

unimagined. It makes claims upon people in an entirely different way from formerly. The Church should have objectively adjusted itself to this situation, in order to offer help to people in the frightening immensity of their problems and to interpret *the meaning of being a Christian* in the face of these new conditions. What new tasks the Church could have undertaken for the new type of youth and of working women! But here also the Church, except for praiseworthy exceptions, *rested immovable on an outworn basis* which—though under entirely different conditions—had established itself in the past.

6. Modern civilization, with its gigantic extensive and intensive development of schools of all grades, with the tremendous expansion of the Press—from the daily Press to the illustrated weeklies—with its external comfort and its broadening of cultural demands, has created for the Word of the Church an audience—if an audience at all—which no longer responds or could respond as in earlier centuries to the outmoded methods of proclamation and teaching. The person of to-day is worn down by a thousand attractions; he is completely saturated by the mass of reading and listening that is at his disposal. It might have been expected that the Church would take counter-measures to meet this terrific aggravation, through the form of its worship services, in its sermons and its methods of instruction. This has indeed happened almost instinctively to a limited extent, but nowhere consciously and according to a plan, nowhere in commensurate degree.

7. The Church has taken small notice of the tremendous increase in population and the even more visible concentration of the population in the large cities. In the seventeenth century a Lutheran pastor complained that in his city there were only seventeen ministers for eleven thousand people. How could one be shepherd and minister to such a congregation? This numerical relation which for him was unbearable has by now become seven or eight times worse in most of the larger centres, even though conditions have become not easier, but unimaginably more complicated, and the individual is no longer set in defined and natural social organisms. How can one be surprised, therefore, if any

spiritual ministry to individuals is entirely unknown to the majority of the people? Instead of the Church dedicating its entire attention to this predicament and seeking to solve the problem of the cure of souls with entirely new means, it has so handled this question that the role of personal ministry to the average Christian has entirely disappeared from his consciousness. Precisely this personal ministry would have been the kind of proclamation which would have been best suited to an atomized society and could have dealt most effectively with the complexity of general conditions and with chaotic inner disunity. But instead of this, the personal approach is what has been outstandingly neglected, apparently on the ground of an understandable feeling on the part of the ministers that they are not up to this responsibility. But the Church should have taken the opposite position: here is a problem which must be tackled and organized in a new way. Above all, the most natural deduction would have been that an effort should be made to break up our *monster Church jurisdictions in the cities*; but this conclusion, which one would take for granted, has been wrecked on the opposition of Church officials and even of ministers, out of senseless motives of prestige.

8. But even if we disregard the breakdown in the concept of the Christian demand upon the individual as one among "a priesthood of all believers," and leave aside the smallness in number of ministers with the one-sided preparation *given* for the work of the ministry, there still remains the evil fact that the Churches have at their disposal no proper instrument for the enlistment and selection of their future ministers. They leave to chance the question as to who should offer himself for the service of the Church. The Church takes into its service whoever gets past the two sieves of the preparatory and theological examinations. It has not yet occurred to people that it is somewhat strange for a Church of Jesus Christ, in the *choice of its workers*—the only really active workers it gives itself—to set up exclusively intellectual criteria, and even these in accordance with a certain concept which held the field at the time of the Reformation! It is no wonder that the ministry as a whole confronts problems which it is in no way competent to

handle, entirely apart from the piling up of problems which the individual minister seldom, and the majority never, are prepared to undertake.

At the conclusion of this critical analysis, let me say that in accusing the Church, we are accusing ourselves. If the Church has slept, so have we all slept, and we who in a very special way should be the watchmen of the Church have been especially irresponsible. I place myself all along the line under the judgment of this analysis of the causes of our predicament.

And now what? If I make bold, in what follows, to set forth certain postulates which seek to show the practical way to improvement, certainly this does not suggest that I consider myself able to meet our evil plight in its totality. These propositions constitute only a beginning in a process which will require time and in which the most competent people must take active part.

PROPOSALS

1. It may well seem questionable whether the recovery of the Church can be brought about in the main by its *official leaders*; but there is no doubt that this is one place where it must start.

(*a*) First of all, the Church must concern itself with better recruiting, both positively and negatively. It should take initiative—as is done in a widespread way and with good results in America—in placing before both young people and parents, through word and pen, the significance of professional Christian service. Especially to-day, and particularly where we have a surplus of theological students, this could best be done without the danger of misunderstanding, under the slogan—quality, not quantity. Above all else, the Church should begin to be selective. In place of the present system, the Church should institute a thorough examination by interview for every prospective theological student at the beginning of his study, to determine his aptitude for the ministry. Such an examination should be of a deeply personal and sympathetic character and its result should be communicated only in the form of earnest counsel.

(*b*) The Church must make an effort to institute varied kinds of ministerial training, even in the framework of the present system, which would, of course, presuppose that a corresponding differentiation of types of ministerial service should be inaugurated. This should apply particularly in regard to religious instruction in higher education and to special work with young people.

(*c*) The Church must make a fundamental change in the manner of training regular ministers. At present a training in theology as a science is our only concern; the spiritual-social area, and the area relating to the distinctive practical functions of the Church, except for the most stepmotherly treatment of practical theology, are almost entirely ignored.

I would regard as ideal a combination which would bring the university and the seminary, the scientifically theological and the spiritually social, to a certain degree into balance. The creation of a "Preachers' Institute," to come at the end of the strictly theological study, could be attempted as a means of transition to this ideal. This, however, would be only an emergency expedient.

(*d*) But even the strictly theological preparation itself must be radically revised. It is now abstractly scientific and too one-sidedly historical. To be sure, a pastor cannot have enough of such knowledge; but if this prevents him from securing other things that are more important, the good becomes the enemy of the best. The theological training of to-day is not a very good schooling in the bringing of the gospel of Jesus Christ to modern man. The equipment for the practical tasks of the Church, not simply through the sermon and religious instruction, but at least as much through the cure of souls and missionary contact with people, is decidedly lacking. I make bold to say this as a teacher of practical theology.

(*e*) No one should become a full-fledged minister without at least two years of experience as an assistant with a modest stipend. We may take medicine as an analogy, in which a period of assistantship is required after the full period of university study. In general it would be desirable that no one should become a pastor below a certain age-limit, which surely should not be below twenty-three years.

(*f*) There should be compulsory and regular courses of study to keep ministers alert, except where voluntary organizations for this purpose already exist, and a special commission of theological professors and ministers should be created to bring this about.

2. There should be a *rebuilding of the system of Church-wardens* from a purely administrative body to a spiritual-ministerial group; a group that should be divided into elders and deacons in accordance with the Reformed pattern.

3. The existence of *sectional parties* within any Synod which is patterned according to the system of political parliaments, is a derision of the Church. The necessary grouping together of people of equal standing and the justifiable expression of their viewpoints must be accomplished in some way that does not completely contradict the character of the Church as community. Anyone who has attended the great synodical meetings in some Protestant countries knows that the demand for a churchly as against a secular concept of the Synod is not utopian. But first of all we must create an awareness of the present intolerable situation.

4. The *mobilization of laymen* is probably the most important of all the measures we would propose, but it can only be carried through when something happens among the clergy along the lines of our first proposals above.

(*a*) The very concept of "laymen" is misleading, both because of its Roman Catholic origin and because it is an anachronism in the modern situation. To these so-called laymen belong university professors, members of government, doctors, writers, journalists; in other words, people who are at least the equals of the ministers in education and knowledge, and who are, therefore, if they are genuine Christians, just as well qualified to serve the Church as are those who have prepared for a special type of service in the Church through theological training. The Church permits these tremendous resources of power to lie fallow; yet it should not only be using, but awakening them. The ecumenical movement has rendered pioneer service in this regard through the co-opting of non-theological experts for particular problems of the Church, primarily in the area of Christian social ethics. Here are great possibilities and tasks: the creation of a Christian journalism, a Christian literature, a Christian philosophy and other spiritual sciences, the laying of foundations for a Christian politics and economics.

(b) The need for individual spiritual ministry can be satisfied, under to-day's numerical conditions, only by the drawing in of extra-official helpers.

The difficulties are chiefly of a more practical nature: are there enough suitable people who have the time? There are already many lay ministers who accomplish a great deal in the cure of souls alongside their own occupations. There are in particular many women who are not only qualified to do such work but who do have the time.

(c) Church members could and should also *be mobilized* for simpler but equally important tasks in the service of the Church; visitation in the homes of new members of the congregation; various types of colportage—what a rôle was played by Bible colportage during the Reformation!— visitation of the sick, cultivation of neighbours. Beginnings in these directions have been made, but only sporadically and timidly. Small Bible study circles is another area, of which we shall speak forthwith.

(d) In the mobilization of laymen nothing is more important than the creation of cells and the cultivation of Christian fellowship. Luther provided the watchword and developed the basic ideas for this aspect of the Christian life in his German Mass. Unhappily, the Church later contested the creation of such groups as smacking of conventicalism. We can no longer afford the luxury of such opposition any more than we can afford the luxury of ignoring the matter. Rather we should give it most emphatic promotion. The abyss between the Sunday sermon and the six days of the week must be filled; the Church must become again a community, not only invisible, but visible.

The creation of cells or study circles, particularly since the Group Movement, is under way within the life of the Church itself and partly in connection with the official duties of the minister. Practical interpretation of Holy Scripture, with exchange of personal experience, brotherly admonition and consolation, *mutua conversatio et consolatio fratrum*, that is the slogan under which Luther incorporated this problem in his Schmalkald Articles, his only confession. In Reformed circles Wesley undertook and accomplished something similar.

Here also schooling is necessary, and in the general manner of the Sunday-school monitor system. The pastor, preferably together with a few experienced non-theologians, provides the leaders of such cells every week with a "preparation," or a didactical treatise on a particular Biblical passage, and the leaders communicate this to their respective circles.

5. When the Church finally recognizes its new situation as *missionary*, it must orient itself not only towards the care of the congregation, but above all else towards its *missionary responsibility*. (See Note on p. 99.—Ed.)

(*a*) The present Sunday-school worship services are burdened by the effort to be at the same time missionary and yet within the congregation. In this combination neither aspect is allowed to come into its own. We must therefore first of all take seriously the fact that there are two kinds of people: Christians, who are certain of their faith in the God revealed in Jesus Christ and in His salvation; and non-Christians, who either believe nothing at all or have a religious faith which is not Christian. We ourselves cannot distinguish these two types of people with certainty, although the confession of faith is at least a provisional relative basis of differentiation. He who confesses the opposite of the Christian faith cannot be counted as a part of the Church, even if he is externally a member.

But this distinction should not lead us to a parting of the ways. The chief question is whether we address ourselves to the two problems with the methods which are respectively valid for them. That is exactly what the ancient Church did. It had different arrangements for the "hearers" who were not yet Christians, and for the actual believing congregations. The Lord's Supper, for example, clearly belongs only in the congregation of the faithful, not in missionary activities. The same holds true for liturgy. There is no liturgy in the mission, because there is as yet no praying congregation. There is also no hymnody, because there is no congregation praising God. We must develop a method of proclaiming the Word which will lead to belief, to the Bible, to the life

96

of prayer; and this should be sharply distinguished from the proclamation to those who already confess Jesus Christ with heart and voice. The first will have no different content from the second, but a different form. It will not be in the technical sense Biblical exposition, as this belongs where people believe in the Bible as the Word of God. Rather, it will proclaim the gospel of Jesus Christ in a form which will meet the understanding and arouse the consciences of those who are far from this truth.

On the other side, if the worship service of the congregation is freed from the attempt to make it at the same time a missionary service, it can conform to a much higher standard, appropriate to a congregation of confessing Christians. One can go deeper into Bible study and even enlist the active participation of the congregation in the service through congregational reading of Scripture, united spoken prayer, responsive readings, and so on. It is here that the hymn has its true significance, similarly the treasures of the liturgy of the early Church. It is here that a truly Churchlike atmosphere can be created.

(*b*) A great difficulty is the vacuum between Sunday and Saturday. The time of the Reformation was familiar with the daily service of worship. This we must have again, even though we might have to select for this purpose a less elaborate form in order not to overburden and exhaust the minister. Daily morning and evening devotions in a simple form would not be impossible either in the city or in the country. Why should we leave to the Romans the advantage they possess in their daily celebration?

(*c*) There exists a tremendous need for true Christian schooling, in the Catechism as well as in the Bible. The usual form of "Bible hour," half preaching and half teaching, is not sufficient to meet this need.

(*d*) Our celebration of the Lord's Supper is in need of much reform. Most people feel that it is unsatisfying in its present form, because the sense of a fellowship meal is not really conveyed. But I do not desire at this point to enter into details.

6. We do not have in the Protestant Church as I know it what might be called a *Christian home library*, but the Swiss

publishing house, Zwingli-Verlag, has spontaneously seized on this suggestion and is extending invitations for a competition to create such a library. I have in mind small, widely understandable booklets which would contain the necessary accoutrement for a Christian life, in so far as the printed word has this power. Thus:

A short introduction to the Bible, together with references to Bible readings.
A guide to prayer, with some really good sample prayers.
A catechism for adults.
A short Church history (naturally, not just a dry compendium).
A booklet on being a Christian: containing the most important directions for family devotions, the Christian attitude on sexual morality and sex relations in general; concerning marriage, the relation of the Christian to money, to pleasure, to the State and to political questions.

The Catechism should not have to be burdened with these matters, and on the other side the treatment of these practical things should not be confined to the necessary limits of a catechism. Perhaps it would be good to handle the separate problems as separate books. In all of this, however, *moral truisms would have to be carefully avoided*. The books would have to speak with realism and competence.

7. The most far-reaching means of preaching which we have at our disposal—namely, *the Radio and the Press*—are usually left to accidental chance. A Church Radio and Press committee should be commissioned, aided by constant contact with the strategic people of the country, to secure the greatest possible publicity for outstanding achievements. Only the best preachers should be permitted to express opinions on the radio, and it is immaterial whether they are situated in a metropolis or somewhere else. The committee should pay attention to no special interests, whether they be regional or theological. A few men enjoying fullest confidence should comprise this committee and be given full power, including that of the theological direction referred to.

Herewith I come to the end of my propositions. I am aware

of the discrepancy between the presentation of our plight and the interpretation of its causes. It is unavailing to try to obviate the most important dangers merely by bringing forth propositions. And many postulates have no significance until others have already been fulfilled. Yet I believe, nevertheless, that the connection between the postulates and the analysis is visible at every point and that the postulates all live up to the condition that one must always place upon postulates: they should not be utopian but realizable demands, even though their fulfilment might require a long time. This much is clear: *things dare not simply continue as they have been in the past*. The Church must make a start and stir itself to earnest measures for improvement. It looks, for example, as though our Swiss people will need more bitterly than ever in the years ahead the courageous mighty help of the Church. May God find us, not as faithless slumberers, but as true and watchful servants.

NOTE: *Dr. Brunner's fifth Postulate introduces the contemporary conception of an "Inner" and an "Outer" Mission within the Church's sphere of responsibility. The former will be referred to later here towards the close of Miss Owen's contribution, pp. 124–5. Its reference there is to the current German usage, namely the "area of Christian charity." In Scandinavia, however, the phrase belongs to the ministry of the Word and not of the hand. That is to say, it equates with Brunner's spiritual upbuilding of the faithful within the worshipping congregation. Scandinavia has the term* diakonia *to cover the sphere of Christian charity.*

Presumbly the "Outer Mission" could cover both what we generally refer to as "Home Mission" in Britain, and also the fuller extension of the Church's responsibility, the "Foreign Mission."—ED.

Gospel and Law: Punishment of War Criminals

by

F. B. WELBOURN

Student Christian Movement

I HAVE for some time been concerned about the attitude to war criminals expressed in public by both political and ecclesiastical leaders in this country. What follows is reprinted from the *Christian News-Letter* of November 3, 1943. The postscript was added in December.

The need to make decisions on this point is made urgent by the fact that the United Nations' Commission for the Investigation of War Crimes has been established.[1] Of the legal issues, it is better for the layman to be silent. There is a valuable account in "War Crimes and the Problem of an International Criminal Court,"[2] by Georg Schwarzenberger; and responsible legal opinion now thinks that such crimes can be dealt with by existing national and military courts. But the fact that, once a state of war ceases, their case is covered by no existing international law, means that the problem is political rather than legal, and leaves room for considerable Christian initiative in the creation of a sound public opinion, which may go far to determine the relevant clauses of an armistice and the ultimate formulation of international law.

GOSPEL AND LAW

In order to think this question effectively, it is necessary to make a distinction between two spheres of action—of gospel and law, of love and justice—in which, however

[1] And more recently (April, 1944) by the vindictiveness of the Algiers trials, which are a measure of what we may expect elsewhere.

[2] Reprinted, under the auspices of the Czechoslovak Branch of the International Law Association, from the "Czechoslovak Year Book of International Law," 1942, pp. 67–88.

unclearly he may see their boundaries, the Christian has to act. In the first—largely that of his personal relations—he is faced with the absolute demands, made by God's act in Christ, of unconditional forgiveness towards wrongdoers. In the second, precisely because he is a Christian, recognizing secular society as the potential sphere of God's rule, he has an overwhelming responsibility to co-operate with all other elements in that society towards the creation and maintenance of a social order which is, within the limits of historical possibility, just.

This is the sphere in which our Lord refused to adjudicate ("Who made me a judge or divider over you?" Luke xii. 14), because there is no ultimate solution except in terms of forgiveness. Neither can the Christian here make ultimate judgments, knowing the tragic double-sidedness of all human action in society. But, knowing also the infinite possibilities, under God, of every situation, he cannot refuse the responsibility of relative judgment and action as a citizen. And, in the exercise of that responsibility, he will use the gun, the gallows or the gaol, if the needs of an ordered society seem to demand them.

There are two opposite, but equally dangerous, errors inherent in the ease with which the two spheres of gospel and law can be confused. The first is that we should try to apply the demand for unconditional forgiveness between persons to the sphere of order in a secular society. Of that enough has been said in other places. Its acceptance would exclude Christians from responsible co-operation in the maintenance of social order.[1] And, although there is a strong case to be made against the use by Christians of legal machinery for their own protection, it seems to me that our responsibilities as citizens can be renounced, if at all, only when we have abandoned all hope of useful co-operation.

In illustration, perhaps I may be allowed to quote a personal problem which faced me, some eighteen months ago, when I was forced to the conclusion that I was using my privileged position of unconditional exemption from combatant service as an escape from making a definite

[1] I take this to be essentially Mr. Stephen Hobhouse's position, expressed in "Retribution and the Christian," Fellowship of Reconciliation, 2d.

decision about the challenge of pacifism. The issue—as, rightly or wrongly, it presented itself to me—entailed the decision between, on the one hand, dissociating myself, so far as possible, from modern civilization by joining a pacifist community; and, on the other hand, becoming—despite the time-honoured tradition of clerical non-combatancy, which, up till then, I had strongly maintained—a combatant member of the Home Guard. I chose the latter.

It may well be that, in so doing, I was seeking to escape from a tension which is inherent in the life of the priesthood. If so, it was an escape only into a new tension—the world-long tension between the relative demands of social necessity and the absolute demands of God in Christ. For there is no absolute justification of combatancy without the identification of the Allied and Axis powers, respectively, with the hosts of heaven and of hell. And just this is the second danger of confusion between the spheres of gospel and law: that we should be psychologically incapable of fulfilling the stern demands of the law unless we persuade ourselves that they are absolute; that we should forget that all human action is relative and falls short of the love of God. If we do that, we renounce our obligation to bring the law under the reforming power of the gospel.

Under this head, I believe, fall recent Christian attempts to distinguish between retribution and revenge, as motives in the treatment of war criminals. It is all too easy to conceal an unworthy motive by giving it a respectable name. Allied policy towards war criminals, as at present expressed in "Punishment for War Crimes,"[1] and in Mr. Eden's statement in the House of Commons,[2] is, and must necessarily be, in the sphere of law; and, as such, it requires, and can seek, no absolute justification. But Christians can make their proper contribution to the formulation of such a policy only if they are first clear as to the attitude of the gospel towards wrongdoers. And I shall, therefore, try to state what I believe that attitude to be before considering the political situation in the light of the insights which it gives.

[1] H.M. Stationery Office, 6d. The pamphlet contains notes presented by the governments of the occupied countries to the British, Soviet and American governments and the consequent statements by Mr. Churchill, the Soviet Government and President Roosevelt.
[2] December 17, 1942.

THE GOSPEL OF FORGIVENESS

Of the heinous character of the atrocities which have been committed, nothing need be added to what has already been published in the Press.[1] But that in no way alters the ultimate purpose, as it is revealed in Christ, of God's action towards each sinner. He aims always at redemption, to call out from man the love which is the only true response to His love. And His action is utterly personal, love striving to evoke love through action entirely appropriate to the sinner's condition. If He must punish, the punishment is a language, revealing to the sinner the character of his deed, calling him to repentance and so to a restoration of relationship. God wants the sinner to echo the repentant malefactor ("and we indeed justly," Luke xxiii. 41), to recognize the relation between sin and punishment, and so to put himself in the position where, in the words of the General Confession, he may "turn from his wickedness and live."

There is no suggestion here, as in the Greek tragedies, of a crime abstracted from the criminal and to be expiated by some externally imposed penalty. My attention was drawn to this problem most forcibly by the contrast between the attitude of some Christians, who appear to regard the exaction of penalties for crimes as a duty religiously imposed, and the "scientific attitude" that human conduct (including war crimes) is the product of natural causes, and that the rational consequence of such a view is to search for a cure. This is no place to discuss the large issues which that contrast raises. But it seems to me to throw down a big challenge to Christian thinking. Precisely because we are Christians, we are concerned not with the dead past, but with the creative present, pregnant with possibilities for the future of man in society. And the past enters into our creative thought and action only in so far as it helps us to understand the present and to control the future. Such a view does not necessarily abandon punishment; it simply insists that its use should be relevant to the sinner's need.

[1] See also the annexes to "Punishment for War Crimes (2)."

It may well be that courts of law can make no distinction between the penitent and impenitent criminal, and that both must suffer equally. That is a measure of human weakness; it does not lessen the demands of the gospel. Forgiveness alone, using as its means, if necessary, the sternest punishment, can restore not only the social order but the whole cosmic order, broken through sin. Though, to the impenitent, the action of forgiving love may appear, on the one hand, as mere weakness, on the other hand, as the working of an impersonal retribution: yet the penitent knows that God meted to him the measure he deserved, precisely because forgiveness was his only true desert, and only thus could he be brought to joyful acceptance of the new relationship with God and costly action for the restoration of the order which his sin destroyed. God always longs and strives for the restoration of relationship; and the measure of His punishment is the measure, not of the crime, but of the sinner's need. Repentance brings not only new life and faith for the future, but pardon for the past.

And to that understanding of the nature of God's justice, Christianity adds a further insight. The uniqueness of the Christian attitude lies in the recognition that "while we were yet sinners, Christ died for us" (Rom. v. 8). The judge suffers with and at the hands of the condemned: for that is the guarantee of justice, the way of love and, consequently, the only *effective* way. It is true that it becomes effective only when accepted by the condemned, so that he willingly shares the suffering of the judge. But the judge's action is independent of such acceptance. Love makes no conditions, but is confident of final victory.

Of final victory: for, though many Christians differ, I find it impossible not to agree with St. Paul that "God hath concluded them all in unbelief, that He might have mercy upon all" (Rom. xi. 32). But, in any case, the final judgment of a man's character is in God's hands. He alone can say, in any absolute sense, that a man has finally rejected forgiveness and is worthy of death.

In these terms alone a Christian must judge his action in the sphere of the gospel. First, that he aims always at redemption, at the restoration of true harmony between God and man, between man and man, and in the whole cosmic order. Secondly, that forgiveness alone is truly creative, whether it be expressed in a sternness which risks being mistaken for revenge, or in suffering under wrongdoing which is taken easily for mere passivity. Thirdly, that he shuns no personal suffering which his task requires, even at the risk of apparent failure. And, fourthly, that he never loses faith in the possibilities of any man, leaving the final issue to God.

THE CORPORATENESS OF SIN, AND INDIVIDUAL RESPONSIBILITY

A further important insight into the present issue is given by the Christian understanding of the corporate nature of sin. In "Father Zozima's Biographical Notes,"[1] there is a cogent passage which we should all do well to take to heart:

> "No one can judge a criminal until he recognizes that he is just such a criminal as the man standing before him, and that he perhaps is more than all to blame for that crime. When he understands that, he will be able to be a judge."

We have all sinned, and the sins of each promote the sins of all. The Nazi doctrine of corporate responsibility is a reversion to the primitive insight, which recognized the responsibility of every member of a family, or village, or tribe for the crimes of its individual members. And, because it is a reversion, it is rightly condemned as barbarous.

But the modern, and exceedingly important, emphasis on the responsibility of each for his own actions still falls short of the truth; and it becomes a dangerous half-truth, if it is applied indiscriminately, without regard for mitigating circumstances. Man is one in sin, if in nothing else. And the current analysis of the political and economic causes which ended in war add nothing but detail to a fact which all Christians should have known from the start. Although the sin of all comes to a focus and finds active expression in

[1] Dostoievski, "The Brothers Karamazov," Book VI, Chapter II (h).

unfortunate individuals, ultimately we are *all* responsible for this war; we are *all* responsible for the crimes to which it has given rise—the extermination of the Jews and all the other atrocities of the Hitler régime. To these, as to all crimes, the genuine Christian response is *mea culpa, mea maxima culpa*—repentance in dust and ashes, followed by energetic and costly action to right such wrongs as are not beyond repair.

ACTION UNDER LAW

But what, within the sphere of the law, is that action to be? Here our responsibility, as citizens, is for the creation of a just international order; and our major concern, so far as in us lies, must be the prevention of future wars. To this are closely linked, on the one hand, the issues raised in the Beveridge Report; and, on the other hand, the necessity which is laid on us, both as Christians and as wise citizens, of working for the time when Germans may play their full part in the comity of nations. Those questions I have neither the space nor the competence to discuss. But it is certain that there is no practical answer to them, except in a willingness for economic and political sacrifice by the allied nations, to which, perhaps, only a Christian faith is adequate.

The important distinction between "Germany and the Hitlerite State" has already been made by M. Stalin[1] and debated at length in the House of Lords.[2] But, as Christians, we desire also that individual war criminals shall have their part in the future. Within the framework of a general international policy, by which Germans would be compelled, indeed, to return stolen treasures, but actively helped to achieve economic and political responsibility in world affairs, war criminals would be retained in labour units set to the physical rebuilding of Europe, and undergoing instruction, education and discipline designed to fit them for free membership of normal society. But against such a plan must be set certain important political objections.

1. The possibility must be faced that a hard core of war criminals will be in no mood to reform their ways, or to

[1] December 6, 1942. [2] March 10, 1943.

106

regard the most lenient detention as in any sense better than revenge. In that case, the immediate problems of reconstruction may well be so vast that such men must be imprisoned, or even shot. And the shooting must be done with as much determination as we now wage war. But we shall not imagine that, in so doing, we are executing the demands of an eternal justice.

2. Some of the best friends of Germany believe that she has developed the tradition of "being able to get away with anything." And one of the major tasks, in the prevention of future wars, is to eradicate that tradition. Legal trials, followed by harsh sentences on a carefully defined class of criminals, would be an important contribution to that task. The allied governments are fortunately determined that, so far as they can ensure, such trials and sentences shall be legally executed. We need not worry our heads about that. But it may be argued that what appears to allied tribunals as the impartial administration of justice will, to the recipients of punishment if not to their compatriots, appear as stark revenge. Against that, it can be said with a good deal of confidence that the majority of Germans are heartily sick of their present rulers and the Nazi underlings, and would gladly see an end of them.

This is a far more cogent argument than that which hopes that punishment for crimes of this war will deter potential criminals in future wars. Only the strong likelihood of being brought to trial—such as exists in a stable society—can have that deterrent effect. And war, such as we are now experiencing, represents a social instability which makes the future course of justice wholly uncertain. Only an international authority, with sufficient power to nip in the bud fresh acts of aggression, could supply the certainty of justice. And, if aggression is checked, there is no war, and no war crimes to deter.

3. Whatever policy is finally adopted will reflect the views not only of Russia, still officially a non-Christian state, but of non-Christian folk in this country and in the exiled governments of German-occupied countries, whose views may very naturally be warped by the emotional reaction to well-attested atrocities. It is certain that they will demand

the death sentence or other unredemptive punishment, in specified cases. And the only chance of influencing the final formulation of policy lies in the recognition that practical co-operation requires compromise, and a sympathetic understanding of the wrongs endured by members of the allied nations. It is all too easy to forgive what we have not ourselves suffered.

4. There is every reason to expect a spontaneous outbreak of bloody revenge in the occupied countries, as soon as the Germans begin to lose their grip. In so far as such an outbreak may accelerate victory, it is one of the horrors to which we are committed by the very fact of war. But its repercussions in future international bitterness would be incalculable; and, in so far as it is avoidable, it is possible that the timely announcement of sufficiently stern legal measures will prevent or check the tide of unrestrained revenge. I do not believe that this argument holds much force. Nothing but a widespread conviction of love towards enemies, or the intervention of the allied armies, is adequate to the task. And how can the policing armies be here, there and everywhere on time?

5. But there is a more serious possibility that a firm allied policy, made widely known, will deter atrocities during the remainder of the present war. Even that is open to question. For disobedience to the order of a superior in the Nazi State brings immediate punishment. And, in the unlikely event of allied threats reaching the ears of those for whom they are intended, the mere possibility of punishment at allied hands is hardly likely to outweigh the certainty of immediate death at the hands of compatriots. And that consideration applies not only to private soldiers, but to all ranks, except perhaps the highest. It is unrealistic to expect such disobedience from any but moral heroes, acting in obedience to a higher law rather than in fear of punishment.

So long as there is hope of an Axis victory, allied threats have little meaning. And as soon as victory is seen to be in the balance, fear of punishment is likely to lead to more strenuous efforts to avert defeat and more severe repressive measures against those elements in the occupied countries— and in Germany itself—which are regarded as a danger to the Nazi régime. It is for this very reason, some German refugees in this country suggest, that the Nazi government has so far withheld from the German people information about atrocities; that, at the last ditch, they may say: "This is what we have done in your name; you have heard the threats of the United Nations; if you give in now, you will be exterminated."

It is true that the last clause is an exaggeration even of isolated opinions which have been expressed in this country; it in no way reflects official pronouncements. But the skill of Nazi propagandists, in turning everything to their own purposes, emphasizes the need for a clear definition of war crime and its legal consequences. Such a definition, though it might earmark notorious leaders for certain punishment, must still leave room for others to turn from their past wickedness and prove their repentance by revolt—a policy which is already implicit in allied propaganda to Italy. And, if it were made widely known at the moment when Germans as a whole see ultimate defeat to be inevitable, it might go far to promote a general defiance of orders and hasten the internal disruption of the German Army.

OUR TASK

It has been said that "our eyes must be constantly fixed on the constructive, redemptive purpose of creating a new order. If we are to do this we need, in a phrase, *to break the entail*. Evil is self-perpetuating in an endless chain, and the only way of dealing with it is to break the process. What we have to do is to make clear to Germany and the world that our purpose throughout is constructive."

The more I think in these terms of the punishment of war criminals, the more I believe that there are three sound reasons for adopting an unredemptive attitude towards them as individuals—that is to say, for the death sentence or any form of punishment which is not aimed at their reintegration into society. The first two are negative: the necessity to compromise, for the very sake of international order, with the large number of people who will demand uch punishment; and the sheer lack of opportunity, in the post-war chaos, to act otherwise. The third is the positive sociological necessity of eradicating the German tradition of impunity.

It seems to me that, in this situation, our task is to try to ensure that the definition of war crime is genuinely just. And there are two points to bear in mind.

1. The unbiased justice of allied tribunals would be made clear to the world by equally careful investigation of charges made by Axis nationals against members of the allied forces: and the execution of equally severe penalties on those found guilty. It would, in fact, be very surprising if such charges ever came to be made in a court of law. What is important is that any definition of war crime should state clearly that, *if* they were made, they would be fairly considered, without detriment to the accuser. A crime is no less a crime because it is committed by one dear to us. And the knowledge that some of our own people might have to suffer under the same law would perhaps mitigate our judgment of Axis criminals. We cannot, in truth, pretend that the same laws of conduct prevail under the stress of war as in a society at peace.

2. More than anything, there is needed a definition of individual responsibility adequate to the actual situation in Nazi Germany. I have already said that the responsibility of each for his own actions may become a dangerous half-truth. The debate in the House of Lords[1] emphasizes the almost intolerable complexity of assessing responsibility for war crimes—of distinguishing between principals and agents, and of determining the extent to which disobedience to the commands of superior officers may reasonably be expected. The fact that, even under German military law, an inferior acting under orders is responsible if he realizes that the order has a crime for its purpose[2] does not affect the practical issue. The difficulty of such disobedience—as of the expression of criticism of the government in a totalitarian State—even by men who profoundly reject the official philosophy and works, is scarcely yet conceived of in this country. It may even be that, in such circumstances, to carry out an order inefficiently results in less suffering than a blunt refusal,

[1] March 10, 1943.   [2] Schwarzenberger, op. cit., p. 72.

which ensures the execution of the order by one whose subservience to the State is unquestionable. And there is room for considerable use of disciplined imagination as a means of bringing home, to ourselves and to others, the actual conditions of living under Nazi rule. It is simply unrealistic—and therefore unjust—to define responsibility in such a situation as rigidly as, in our own country, we justly do.

That is the most important thing I have to say. Without understanding, we cannot hope to heal.

Postscript

While this article was first in the press, decisions were being taken, at the Moscow Conference between the Foreign Secretaries of this country, Russia and America, which may very well render what I have written largely irrelevant to the immediate issue. But, if in any way it stimulates Christian thinking on the relation between *forgiveness* and *justice*, on the mode of action in the *sphere of law* and on a definition of *responsibility*, it will have served a purpose.

In the meanwhile, an interesting Penguin Special, "The Next Germany," has appeared, written by a group of German socialists in this country, which reinforces the view that there is a "German tradition" to be eradicated—although it confines that tradition to a small class of Germans and denies its hold on the "workers." Whatever the truth of this, the "German tradition" is a vital factor in any realistic political thinking. But that is not to deny the existence of undesirable traditions in allied countries. Indeed, the real danger of victory to this country and to the world is that, in the pride of our very real achievements, we should be content to face the future without any radical change in our national attitudes and policies. As a friend writes: "I feel that the greatest blame attaches to us for not having a democratic system which *worked* to offer as an alternative to Germans who did not want Nazism, but could see no alternative— and by *work* I mean a system with less than 15 per cent. unemployment. The abstract attractions of freedom and justice for others are very little when you yourself are faced with the compulsion of an empty belly."

"The Next Germany" also recognizes the necessity for the punishment of war criminals and hopes that much of this will be undertaken by a hypothetical revolutionary government in Germany itself. Such a solution would be more than welcome; for we have to recognize—what I had previously failed to notice—that anti-Nazis, who, from motives of revenge, would gladly shoot their own war criminals, are more than likely to suspect the same motives for punishment meted out by the Allies. For that reason, and on general political grounds, it is very much to be hoped that, from the moment of victory, Germany will show herself worthy and capable of self-government in the tasks of reconstruction and retribution.

Finally, I want to stress even more strongly, if possible, the difficulty of opposing public opinion—especially when that opinion is backed by all the resources of propaganda and oppression now at the disposal of a strong central government. Anyone who will consider honestly the difficulty of such opposition even in this country—where, on the whole, it is not so enforced—must hesitate before condemning the moral victims of the new totalitarianism on the Continent. We have too long thought of freedom—and therefore of responsibility—in the entirely superficial terms of physical freedom from compulsion or restraint: and have neglected the psychological bonds which hold men together in society and condition their responsibility. When those bonds are of the strength and character produced by the Nazi solution to the decay of the individualist era, and when they are reinforced by the external compulsion made possible by science, we may well ask whether a traditional criminal law or a scientific sociology is the better servant of civilization. And we should be quite clear that both are techniques, between which we judge only in terms of their efficiency for their social purpose; neither one nor the other has any ultimate religious sanction. Our task, as Professor Karl Mannheim[1] is always telling us, is to discover the right forms of freedom and responsibility for the modern world: and then to adopt the techniques which are most suited to them. And stock answers are certain to be over-simplified.

[1] "Man and Society" and "Diagnosis of Our Time," both pub., Kegan Paul.

Can Germany Share in Re-education?

by

PATRICIA OWEN

Christian International Service

WITH the end of the war apparently drawing quickly nearer, there is still much talk of the re-education of Germany, but little unanimity concerning the methods which will be possible, and it may be that there is all too little time to waste if the right background is to be prepared before the need for that re-education comes.

In June, 1942, Lord Addison, in the House of Lords, declared that "there would have to be a long-term control of the German education and of the German financial system," the first part of which statement has been much debated. And in March, 1943, there was published the report by the Joint Commission on Education of the London International Assembly and Council for Education in World Citizenship, under the title of "Education and the United Nations,"[1] a large part of which deals with the question of re-education in post-war Germany. This report surveys the needs, as then seen, of the occupied countries, but the section concerning Germany contains more concrete proposals than that dealing with any other single country. The need for outside control is accepted in the form of a High Commissioner for Education, whose "purpose should be to eradicate the Nazi and militarist influence in education and to inspire, to facilitate and to supervise measures by the German people for their own re-education." But it is also made clear that this work of restoration must come from within and not be superimposed from without.

What are some of the numerous conflicting theories as to what should be done?

One very common one is the proposal that the refugees now in this country should go back, but, apart from the question of the British Government's attitude to such

[1] To be obtained from 11 Maiden Lane, W.C.2, 1*s*.

a proposal, there are other obstacles, and there seem to be at least three points of view among the refugees themselves.

The first group hope to return and serve their country in this way—some from political, some from religious motives, and more will be said of this later.

The second group do not want to return; what they have suffered has often left too deep a mark.

The third group consists of those who would like to go, but do not believe it possible either for themselves or others, and their reasons include the following:

Anti-Semitism was not first manufactured by the Nazis, although it has been fostered and used by them to a degree surpassing even the brutalities of the Inquisition, and therefore it cannot be expected to fade out at once, however complete the fall of Nazism.

A factor that involves all refugees, and not only those who became so on racial grounds, is that the more deeply Germany suffers before the end of the war, the greater will be the gulf between her present population and those of her nation who have lived in the—up to now—comparative safety and ease of this country. Unless there is a very deep humility on both sides, this may be an impassable barrier, making contact between German and German even more difficult than contact between Briton and German, since Britain is an accepted enemy nation.

A suggestion made by Dr. Julian Huxley is the creation of an International Education Office. This would obviously be intolerable if Germany alone were to be subject to it, but is not the problem of re-education in Germany only a special part of the whole problem of the reform of education everywhere? This country is already engaged in debating its own needs, and if the universal nature of the questions involved were actively recognized it might afford a practical opportunity of arousing a spirit of co-operation where otherwise the emphasized stigma of being the black sheep among the nations will hamper such co-operation if sought later on. This is a question for the experts, but it is also one on which all who care for the future of the world and its children should form a carefully thought out opinion.

Another proposal is that the text-books of history for

post-war Germany shall be carefully supervised, but this is open to the same criticism as all outside interference.

But these and other suggestions do not answer or diminish the problem:

"How are those forces within Germany which are fitted to undertake the re-education of the nation to be found? Where are they to be sought? How strong are they after over four years of war and ten of Nazi domination?"[1]

Inevitably one wonders how much is left of the rich heritage of German education at its best. It is good in these days, when we are constantly and forcibly reminded of the perversion of the intellect in the invention of terrible methods of warfare and persecution, to remember such achievements as the great contribution of German science to the world of medicine. While one needs to be on one's guard against easy sentimentalism, it is disastrous to ignore the positive facts on which hope for the future may be based. As Dr. H. Friedeberg has written: "For anyone who has had the opportunity to watch the havoc wrought by the Nazis on scientific pursuits and fine arts since 1933, there cannot be the slightest doubt that all those who survive the destruction of what they had worked and striven for, as well as their pupils and adherents, even if they had of necessity become Nazis in the meantime, will be the first to start the cleansing of the Augean stables of the Nazi filth with an iron broom."

Many of those who, before the Nazis obtained control, had a university education, had to win it through sacrifice on their own and their families' part, and this may be a sign of hope, for the more hardly a privilege is won, the more likely it is to be valued.

How shall the men and women of intellect rise up and regain control? That is impossible to tell, but one thing may be said, which is, that if they know that there is a willingness on the part of their ex-enemies to trust them and to support them in their endeavour to undo the work of Nazi training, they may rise to the occasion with a vigour which they would lack if they were faced with complete scepticism from the start. It is easy to object that if these

[1] In response to this large question, see "Education in Post-War Germany," by Minna Specht, International Publishing Coy., 1s.

people existed they would have revolted long before. Nazi control of education grew so subtly that it already had a stranglehold by the time its purpose became unmistakably clear, and there were many who honestly could see no other way in the beginning. A very vivid picture of this is given in Miss Buller's book "Darkness over Germany," which recounts first-hand stories of conversations with men and women of different occupations in Germany in the years 1933–9, telling of their terrible mental and spiritual conflicts.

We look with hope for a new birth of German education springing from those whose intellectual capacities have been held in bondage through the past ten years. But even if this happens, will it suffice? Would the re-establishment of a liberal education root out Nazism? Could it counteract the years of careful inculcation of the doctrines of Blood and Soil, of the lust for domination, of the sense of a purpose in life—even if this purpose entail the destruction of millions and perhaps the sacrifice of their own lives? Why did Nazism take root and flourish if the old educational system was sufficient?

There seems to be fairly general agreement that above all it is youth that needs re-educating, or rather, in many cases, educating, since one of the Nazis' subtlest ways of infiltration and of taking possession was the gradual increase of physical training, which unostentatiously but effectually elbowed out more and more of the mental training, thus preparing a generation whose bodies are developed at the expense of their minds. There is a picture of what Nazi education means given in Peter Wiener's "German with Tears," which gives much food for thought. As an unnamed correspondent from Luxemburg wrote in the *Times Educational Supplement*:

"How can youth which has never learnt to think, to weigh, and to compare, which has been enslaved without being able to perceive to what dark depths of servility it has been brought, which has been forced into the worship of false gods, of an empty ideology, painted nevertheless in the most glowing colours—how can it resist in the long run such fascination through which it believes it sees the grand highway to the wide horizons of a glorious future?"

116

If we are agreed that man is spirit as well as mind and body, we have the most important clue. In many, Nazism was able to enter in and take possession because there was no positive allegiance of the spirit to resist it. The parable of the man whose soul was swept and garnished contains a universal truth; because that soul remained empty it became the home of seven devils. When Hitler chose the title of "Leader" he showed a shrewd insight into the needs of those who had lost their sense of allegiance to God. Man is innately such that he needs a purpose in life, and that purpose must also be outside himself, and must link him with his fellow men in a common loyalty. All this—and more—Hitler provided, at first professing co-operation with the Church, but by degrees, as his power grew, showing the absolute nature of his claims and educating the children and youth to a full obedience.

We submit that nothing less than Christianity can undo this work—no mere code of ethics, however fine, but the full challenge of the whole Gospel, not only taught in school, but active in the lives of men and women in their day-to-day occupations, business and leisure alike, making that absolute claim on the whole of man's life which brings the Church into inevitable conflict with totalitarianism, but which is also the only possible alternative for men and women who have been trained to lose themselves utterly for an ideal.

Why do we claim Christianity to be the only solution?

First and foremost there is this question of man's loyalty. He is made to be God's child and free servant, but if he either is ignorant of or rejects this, he easily becomes the devil's slave. The history of the Churches' resistance to Nazism, first in Germany, then in the occupied countries, is the finest possible witness to the power of Christ against Hitler. The central truths of a book such as "The Village on the Hill," a story based on fact, are a testimony which cannot be overlooked. Sometimes the resistance has come from the Church's leaders, such as Pastor von Bodelschwingh, who refused to surrender his helpless mental patients at Bethel to "mercy killings," or Cardinal Faulhaber who, in 1938, when all were afraid of helping the Jews because of Nazi threats, went to their aid, providing a lorry to remove religious objects from the Chief Rabbi of Bavaria's synagogue and storing them in his palace. A mob attack instigated by the Nazis failed to move him. Sometimes the resistance comes from the rank and file, such as farmers who have risked their lives to feed and clothe Russian and Polish "slave labour," or 400 Roman Catholic boys who insisted on being granted permission to leave a Hitler Youth camp for Sunday Mass.

In this fight Protestant and Roman Catholic stand together, and here is a further factor which may become part of the foundations of future peace and reconciliation in other spheres.

Another reason for the claim made for Christianity is the historical and world-wide nature of the Church. It is, in spite of all its failings, a fellowship into which men may be drawn, and which binds them together despite all barriers. It is a living organism which still links men of warring nations after four years (and in the case of China and Japan longer still) of bitter hostilities. Once again, as with education, in this setting the problem of Germany is seen as part, however vast a part, of the whole problem of the world.

Christianity is a way of life, and upon its faith and its ethics is founded all that is best in our modern civilization. Here is the alternative to the achievements of Nazism in the field of social work and reform, one of the platforms most successfully used by Hitler in the early days of his power. And above all, there is the Christian doctrine of forgiveness which is the one hope for reconciliation in face of the untold horrors of the past years. This is sometimes criticized as though it were an easy dismissal of wrongs done to others, but the statement recently issued by Christian leaders in Norway concerning the post-war treatment of war criminals brings witness from a quarter where suffering has been acute. It concludes: "The Church desires settlement—not laxity, justice—not revenge, reconciliation—not hatred." This doctrine is the only one which adequately meets the case, because it faces the fact, not only of Germany's sin against mankind, but of man's sin against God.

How much can we count on the presence in Germany of those who can undertake the necessary work of re-education?

In answering this query, a distinction must be borne in mind between the problem of re-education generally and that of Christian education such as is referred to above. For there are important non-Christian elements which may help in the work of general re-education. Details of the Underground Movement are scarce, but it is almost certain that at least a large proportion of its members are socialist or communist, whose resistance to Hitlerism is political. There are those in this country who are planning to make contact with them at the earliest opportunity to help them to free their nation from Nazism by replacing it with their own doctrines.

In this connection, one of the biggest uncertainties concerning the whole post-war period may be mentioned—namely Russia's intended policy towards a conquered Germany. Always bearing in mind the possibility of great changes, indications up to date show that while there may be heavy reprisals on "war criminals," there may also be a powerful attempt to win the German nation to the Russian ideology.

But we are above all concerned with the question of the Church's part in re-education.

In a recent letter to *The Times*, Bishop Fyffe writes:

". . . What is needed is not outward organization of Germany, but a change of heart in Germans. That can best—perhaps only—be achieved by setting free the religious bodies in Germany to take as large a part as they can in the education and other youth work of their country. To give this freedom must surely be the first duty of the victorious Allies, as it is the most fundamentally important thing they can do in Germany and for Germany. If the religious bodies take the opportunity offered to them the reform of Germany will have come from within and therefore may endure."

And in "Christian Counter-attack"[1] the chapter on Germany ends:

[1] S.C.M. Press

"No one can tell what will ensue as the prospect of military defeat becomes more and more vivid to all ranks within Germany. We must not rely on any kind of political revolution from the German Confessionals. The very strength of their conviction comes from their belief that Christianity is not concerned with politics. . . . What we can say, however, without risk of contradiction, is that there is in Germany a considerable element in the Evangelical Church which understands Nazism at least as well as we do, has suffered bitterly through resisting it, and is deeply attached to the essential truths of the Christian religion. There should be some possible ground of future collaboration in this undeniable fact."

If these Christian elements are to take the lead, how strong are they? Active numbers in the Confessional and other resisting Protestant and Roman Catholic Churches can only be guessed, but the points to be considered in making one's guess are sometimes hard facts.

On the one hand the numerical strength of the Church has been consistently diminished by murder, the concentration camp and death at the front. Out of some 18,000 Evangelical pastors 1,300 have been arrested at one time or another since 1934, over one-third have been called up, and as early as April, 1942, in an official report, the number of those killed at the front was given as 698. Roman Catholic priests were not at first called up, but thousands have suffered in prisons and concentration camps, often for what the Nazis termed "speaking disloyally" about the State, or, in other words, denouncing the totalitarian claims of Nazism.

On the other hand, the very number of those attacked or removed witnesses to the strength of the Church's life, which, far from giving in, rather grows in vitality. To quote again from "Christian Counter-attack":

"Perhaps one of the main ways in which the Confessional Church still resists anti-Christian Nazism is by its quiet perseverance in Christian pastoral work. This is having an effect. The Christian way of life as a practical alternative to the Nazi world power is being taken seriously even in unexpected quarters. It is not unknown for youths in S.A.

and S.S. uniforms to attend religious meetings and ask intelligent questions. The calling-up and arresting of pastors has led to a striking development in the lay ministry. The ministry of women is also being pushed forward within certain limits."

There are also indications that Christian confirmation means much more to-day than a generation ago, when, as so often in this country, it represented a kind of social qualification. This is due to the realization that Christian teaching answers certain questions which National-Socialism cannot answer. Catechetical instruction has consequently found a new significance.

Another indication of the new life and understanding in the Protestant Church is the growth of instructional classes such as are described in "The Village on the Hill" or in Pastor Ehrenberg's "Autobiography of a German Pastor." The pastor says:

"These instruction classes had a wider field, however; training in seeing the value of the Church's witness. For this it wasn't necessary to be a theologian; nor was there any need to be embarrassed by possessing little aptitude for theology. We found that the timid people were usually intellectuals who preferred a sentimental kind of Christianity. Here in England much surprise is expressed at the fact that people with little education had a better understanding of the nature of the Church than the members of the more educated classes, especially in the difficult questions of belief, when the struggle was at its height.

"I wonder what Christians outside Germany would say if they knew what we did at these classes, if they could imagine the difficult tasks to which we applied ourselves, working at the articles of the Augsburg Confession for months at a time, hard enough as they often are, so as to be well equipped to deal with the pseudo-beliefs which the heretics wanted to superimpose on our religion?"

What then is the conclusion so far?

Re-education cannot successfully be imposed from without, even by returned refugees, but must come from within

Germany. Those elements which may provide the men and women for this task are to be sought in the Underground Movement, which is largely political, and in the Christian Churches. We believe that the latter alone can offer the full solution to the problems created by Nazism and total warfare.

But it is doubtful whether there are sufficient men and women for the task, for those who are spiritually and mentally qualified may often be physically weakened by years of oppression, perhaps in concentration camps, and will need time to recover health before taking their part in the rebuilding of their nation as a peaceful member of the world comity of nations.

What then? How are the hands of those who may first attempt the work to be strengthened?

The first need is a right attitude in this and other countries. Let it again be emphasized that sentimentalism is to be deprecated. The full evil of Nazism needs to be seen to be combated; added to which the nations which have suffered most severely will not rest until justice has been meted out, and we can only pray and plan that "justice" may not become unbridled vengeance. But even while the punishment is dealt there must be the creative expectation that will help the people of Germany to reconstruct their life as a co-operating force in the life of the world. There is a wise saying in Kipling's "Jungle Book": "One of the beauties of the Jungle Law is that punishment settles all scores. There is no nagging afterward."

But beyond this again there lies a need. We must approach it with a caution because there is so much talk about the re-education of Germany which implies that we can go and "re-convert" them without a thought of the reforms needed in our own land. And this again leads to a natural revolt from the idea that anyone from this country should think of going over there, however humbly.

Having said that, we must face this question: If events prove that the best elements in Germany need numerical strengthening—they may not, but they may, and if they do— is it presumptuous to seek to be prepared for any request that they may make? If they turn only to neutral, largely

Lutheran or Reformed, countries, Sweden and Switzerland, then we cannot intrude. But if they also turn to us in the desire for reconciliation and that the gulf may be bridged, can we be prepared to meet them?

One can only guess at the kind of opening that might come. If English is still taught in schools, perhaps here may be one possibility; if the Church sees as part of its task the rebuilding of relationships it may find a means to welcome here and there one who comes with a desire to serve. There may be a need for trained gifts to help in physical reconstruction after the needs of the occupied countries have been met. But whatever the call may be, if one come at all, it must come to people who are prepared, and the preparation is alike for all, involving not only the mastery of the German language, but a working knowledge of the whole background; history, literature, art, culture, political economy, theology, and other common beliefs, and Church life. Also it means thinking out afresh one's own belief. This is not a mere intellectual exercise; it is a vital part of the understanding of another people.

This can only be justifiably advocated if there is a clear perception of the utter uncertainty of the great effort involved in such preparation being of service in the desired way. But if the risk be seen and accepted willingly, then there will be no loss, for should the opening never come, yet the knowledge won may in itself be of real service, for it will help to form that clarity of thought which is necessary not only in wartime, but in peace, to lessen the factors which make for war. And if in years to come holidays abroad once more become feasible, it may be possible to go as visitor where one was not able to go as a worker, and one more link in the chain of friendships may be forged.

There is yet another consideration which affects the whole people of this country. Some may object to such ideas as have been put forward that all depends on the attitude of the government in power when the moment comes. But this nation is called a democracy and its people can have a large say in its policy when they choose. Therefore it is imperative that an informed public opinion upon these vital questions should be growing now. The Commission which produced "Education and the United Nations" states the question clearly:

"Education in any country is conditioned by the whole life of the country and the major interests it pursues. Therefore, in the last analysis, the possibilities of re-education in Germany and the nature of that re-education will depend upon issues far outside the scope of this report. The absolute power of the United Nations will give them a decisive influence on the development of internal conditions in Germany, and upon the policy they pursue towards Germany will depend the possibility of there emerging a new German state, with such social and economic conditions as will enable it to provide for all its people, without distinction of class or creed, a fuller and happier life of peaceful development and service to the community and the world at large than they have ever known before. Only in so far as the German people have grounds to hope for such a future will they be able to re-educate themselves as good citizens of Germany and of the world community."

With something of all this in mind, a movement started on a small scale in 1941. It was concerned not only with the problem of relations with Germany, but also friendship with other countries as well—particularly stressing the desirability of service, and, where possible, the humblest forms of service. It has grown and developed in sometimes unexpected ways, under the name of Christian International Service. Its members are of widely differing types and occupations, and their aims concerning service are varied, but one common desire links them all. There are nurses who would like to offer their services for work in "Inner Mission" or other hospitals; women trained or training for social work of different kinds; teachers ready to offer their gifts, not necessarily for teaching, but to help in caring for the thousands of children who may be orphaned; men and women in the Forces who may be part of an army of occupation; Civil Servants who may be used in their ordinary capacity. Others do not hope to go abroad, but know themselves to be part of the Christian public here, and a few would like to open their homes to receive children, should any be brought to this country for restoration to health of body and mind. Some are already tackling languages; others are studying background. But the common desire is to work as Christians for reconstruction and the reconciliation of nations, with the fundamental idea that those who hope to serve in the reconstruction of Germany—or any other nation—need to recognize fully the meaning of the Church struggle (or as fully as is possible to one who has not experienced it personally), for one of the essentials of reconstruction and reconciliation is the principle of give and take, recognizing that both sides have a contribution to make towards the whole. And we who have not been persecuted for our faith will have to bear ourselves very humbly towards those who have.

Amongst the refugees who were referred to as desiring to return there are two experiments to be mentioned:

One is a training house recently opened for those who would like to go back to Germany and Austria to help in the work of the "Inner Mission." They believe that, however many difficulties may have to be faced in this work, God's power is able to overcome them if He wills.

The other experiment is a college for men who wish to train for the Lutheran ministry, also in the hope of returning to help to fill the gaps left by war and persecution.

As representatives of the movements travel the country, they find a lively interest in these problems in many quarters—youth clubs, women's groups, mining communities, university circles, schools. At present this interest is often undirected and vague, but the war has awakened thousands to a new consciousness of the many conflicts which underlie the outward one, and now is the moment to make of this consciousness the foundation for a new understanding between nations, an understanding whose strength is drawn from a common faith, in the richest sense of that word.

"For ye are all the children of God by faith in Christ Jesus. For as many of you as have been baptized into Christ have put on Christ. There is neither Jew nor Greek, there is neither bond nor free, there is neither male nor female; for ye are all one in Christ Jesus."

Can Christianity and Communism Meet?

by

TIRAN NERSOYAN

Chaplain of the Armenian Church, London

THE greatest of all the forces which have gathered strength and are exerting themselves to give the modern world a new orientation is Communism. Whatever the outcome of the present global struggle at the battle points, whoever the eventual military victor, the force which will triumph in the end will be the one which has the greatest inherent energy rooted deeply in the universal needs and aspirations of civilized society as a whole. While Fascism is both historically and philosophically an artificial and reactionary, and therefore a temporary, structure, Communism has all the elements of permanence in it.

Communism is claimed to be the emergence into consciousness of that "historical necessity" which has operated all along the life of mankind. Its guiding principles are derived from a certain interpretation of history which is called Historical Materialism. And this in turn is based on a comprehensive world-outlook, on an all-embracing philosophy, which is Dialectical Materialism. This philosophy represents an attempt to describe the struggle between content and form, substance and essence, quantity and quality, substantive and predicate (all these pairs of terms meaning practically the same thing) in their forward movement of integration.

The importance of Communism must be seen from two different angles. Firstly, it is the form of life of one of the greatest social units in the world. It covers an immense area with unlimited potentialities. Consequently its method of approach to the problems of social life is bound to react on the social life of mankind as a whole. From a Christian point of view, it also affects the life of a great Orthodox Church. Through this Church, Christianity comes into direct contact with it. This "Russian" Communism, which is really that of a multitude of races and cultures forming the Soviet nation, and which had its roots in the Russia of the pre-Revolution period, would not be destroyed even by a military defeat. The work of twenty-five years of education, based on older tendencies in the country, could not be undone in a short period, if at all. Communism has inspired and will inspire a vigorous body of young men and women with high ideals. The missionary zeal of this aggressive force is fired by a faith not born of fancy, not engineered for the ulterior purpose of shaping tools for a fiendish design of international robbery, but created for a grand, almost apocalyptic vision of a future of happiness and peace which will belong to all men.

Secondly, Communism is a supra-national factor. It exists in all nations and countries. The size and the character of various parties in different countries give no indication of its real force. Its importance and weight lie in the fact that the ideas underlying Communism, in their broad outlines, are everywhere "in the air." These ideas form the ordinary common-sense world outlook of the masses. They may sometimes be, countered by individual interests, but they have no serious rival to challenge them on the ideological field. The Communist slogans are easily understood by and appeal to a very large number of people who are sick of the chaos and the misery of the world. The reality of matter and its importance, the reliance upon and devotion to science, intended, as it is, to be utilized for universal human happiness, the obvious inevitability of planning and organization, the principle of the equality of men, the necessity of the struggle against all kinds of oppressions, the sanctity of labour, the providence of the State, realizing the objective unity of society, opportunity and education for all, free cultural development for every nation and race—all these are the common aspirations of ordinary men and women. And Communism stands for them all. It is the logical conclusion of all forms of socialism (the methods of reaching this conclusion and the way and the measure in which the U.S.S.R. has arrived at them, being of secondary importance). It is the journey's end of all social and economic reforms.

Assuming these to be the facts, it is imperative for the Church to take a most serious account of Communism, which presents her with one of the greatest problems of her history.

Up to the present time, Christianity and Communism have generally adopted a mutually hostile attitude, the causes of which are ramified and deep. They can be divided into two classes: ideological and factual. The antagonism on factual grounds is mainly concerned with the past and present activities of either of these institutions. Thus the Church is accused of having been and of still being a reactionary force which has stood in the way of genuine social progress, although she has been of some use culturally. She is accused of having helped the ruling classes to keep the toilers under oppression and subject to exploitation, of having deceived the masses by imaginary other-worldly promises, by making them take flight into phantasy and by cultivating an anti-scientific spirit. In a word, she is accused of being a social superfluity and a parasitical encumbrance. Communists, on the other hand, have been accused by Christians of being suppressors of personal freedom, of upholding a cruel and oppressive dictatorship, of denying the value, the sacredness and the rights of individuals, of going against human nature by artificial regimentation, of stifling the human spirit and thwarting its higher aspirations, of destroying human initiative, of subjecting the spirit of man to economic considerations, of blinding the masses by the false doctrine of materialism.

All these and similar indictments, however, do not carry much weight, because the actions and policies of an organization, varying according to circumstances in different periods, must be judged only on the merit of those principles, basic or derivative, which ultimately supply the justification or explanation of such actions or policies, even if these appear to be reprehensible by themselves. To take one of many instances: the cruelties which were committed during the period of collectivization were not indulged in as a matter of course. They were allowed as being incidental to the urgent necessity of feeding the growing populations of the towns adequately, of regularizing the economy of the country in general and for other practical reasons. They were realistic measures. Or, to take an example from the other side: it is true that the clergy in the Church have very often and to a large extent associated themselves with the ruling classes and have not always been innocent of exploiting the poor and the working people, if we judge by modern socialistic ideas. But even if this is true historically, it does not mean that Christian principles in themselves imply such an attitude as a necessary corollary. It is universally admitted that when the Church began to acquire wealth and was established as a State religion, she lost her primitive purity and singlemindedness, which was the price she paid for unified and integral social life. This perhaps was inevitable in the circumstances. Christianity as such having no political programme of its own, the Church, it may be said, had to comply with the existing political conditions and adapt herself to her worldly environment in order to live at all. But it must not in the meantime be forgotten that she never ceased to resist this conformity. And again, this does not mean at all that slavery or feudalism or capitalism is essentially connected with Church organization.

THE NECESSITY OF A RATIONALISTIC APPROACH

Thus many indictments brought by Christianity against Communism and *vice versa* can be relegated to the domain of secondary and accidental problems. And this leads us to the main and essential question: What are the basic principles which form the permanent foundations of the temporary and changing policies either of the Church or of Communism? It is a question which brings us to the theoretical issues involved. The consideration of the conduct in history of the Soviet State or of the Communist Party or Parties and of the Christian Church or Churches respectively serves no useful purpose for the future unless first a courageous confrontation of Dialectical Materialism and Christian Philosophy is attempted. No history can be intelligible unless the guiding principles of its course at the rock bottom are explored and mapped.

This is why the very first thing to do when approaching Communism must be to compare the Christian and Communist philosophies, which are the mainsprings of the thought and of the behaviour of the Church and the Soviet State respectively. Not that Communists would welcome such a comparison, or any approximation resulting from it. A Communist said to me that such an approach could only be an opportunist measure on the part of the Church to avoid defeat. This suspicion, however, can have no lasting value in itself.

There are two ways of access to religion. One is by understanding in order to believe, and the other is by believing in order to understand. More often than not these two ways run parallel. Judging by the intellectual atmosphere in which the young generation in the Soviet Union has been brought up, it may safely be said that the possibility of the success of a direct, explosive appeal to faith is almost non-existent. As to the broad masses of the people, there can be no approach to them over the heads of the intellectuals. Thus any intelligent contact with the Soviets will have to take the route of rational exposition, of argumentation, taking this word cleansed of its sophistry. In other words, these atheists will have to be induced to understand first. It cannot too often be repeated that a "revivalistic," non-rational evangelization cannot take root in a communistic environment, at least as far as the general policy of such eventual evangelization goes, for "revivalist" appeal succeeds either when the paganism is simply moral or when it is speculative to such an extent that it has no direct relevance to the practical issues of life. Soviet Communism is a highly successful working system.

The argumentation or apologetic which we have in mind can take only one direction. It starts from the premise that matter is reality and that it is basic, that a law immanent to this reality governs the movement of it, and that events in history occur in accordance with the rational pattern of this law. The sequence of the reasoning can be briefly put: Along and through the process of history, reality has increasingly developed and acquired certain qualities. These qualities are of a "spiritual" kind. A reality with spiritual qualities is called spirit. Hence, reality is destined to be changed into spirit. The realization of this destiny is man's mission.

THE PHILOSOPHY OF MATERIALISM

Dialectical Materialism starts with the assertion that "nature is primary" (Engels) in opposition to the primacy of God or of the Idea. "Mind is merely the highest product of matter" (Marx). "We start from real, active men, and then from their life-process show the development of the ideological reflexes and echoes of this life-process" (Marx-Engels). "What individuals are depends on the material conditions of their production" (Marx-Engels). The aim of a materialist is "to comprehend the real world, i.e. Nature and history, just as it presents itself to everyone who approaches it free from preconceived idealist fancies," says Engels, and adds, "and materialism means nothing more than this." Lenin defines the term "matter" thus: "Matter is a philosophical category designating the objective reality which is given to man by his sensations and which is reflected by our sensations while existing independently of them." In order to designate this "objective reality," the word "being" is more often used by materialists.

As to dialectics, it is "the science of the general laws of motion, both of the external world and of the human thought" (Engels). "The great basic thought" behind dialectics is that "the world is not to be comprehended as a complex of *ready made things*, but as a complex of *processes*" (Engels). "The real unity of the world consists in its materiality" (Engels).

Even these few typical quotations show the basis and the general trend of dialectical materialistic thought. It starts with what is given, that is, the objective reality. It aims at understanding it by scientific investigation and by studying the laws of its motion as seen in its process and finally tries to dominate nature progressively and to transform it according to the desires of men, by the methodical application of its own laws. Human beings and society as a whole are part and parcel of nature. They are of it and in it. Man is nature's highest product. The special branch of Dialectical Materialism which studies the process by which society has developed its forms in different periods is the domain of Historical Materialism.

In the first place, it is readily seen that this attitude, which is wholly different from that of mechanical materialism, is the ordinary common-sense as well as scientific attitude. Many scientists may not agree with the elaborations of the detail of such a system of thought. That is immaterial. Dialectical Materialism does not claim to be an exposition of scientific truths. It is a method of approach to reality. It is a belief in certain principles which are seen working in nature and in life.

Secondly, it must be noted that there is nothing inherently anti-Christian in the scheme, as long as it is confined to the temporal order. The primacy of nature or matter is asserted only in the sphere of the temporal order. Materialists insist that matter comes first in time. But time is the sequence of events within the whole of reality, it is a relation of parts. For the whole as such there is no time, except in relation to its own parts. But God is the whole, and time begins with creation, hence matter is indeed first in time. The whole, for materialists, is primary in quality and value. Hence axiologically and logically God is primary, because God is ultimately the whole of reality. Materialists could only object to the word "God" being used. But it is for Christians to define the term. The dialectical process of development is the mode in which reality proceeds in time. If objective observation leads us to realize that that process is the mode in which God exercises His providence, there is no reason why our observation should not be trusted. The God of Christians is not an "idea," nor is He Someone in the clouds. Not only is He "objective reality," but He is also *the* Objective Reality. But the attribute "objective" is the necessary correlative of the term "subjective." Hence He is also subjective at the same time, just as man is in his own limitation. This would be implied in the materialist assertion that "thinking is the attribute of being."

Again, God is not "an extra-mundane creator," as Engels calls Him. He is *the* One Universal Reality, and all particular realities are in Him and He is in them. If being has the attribute of thinking in the instance of human existence, it must be said that the whole of reality must be regarded as having that attribute. If thought is the reflection of the process in reality, as Lenin maintains, then that process must itself have the nature and the quality of thought, otherwise human thought could not be its reflection, which it is.

To proceed a step further: the process which is seen as taking place in reality is a continual process of qualification. Evidently the highest quality yet achieved is seen in man in the form of spirituality, consciousness. A quality, however, is as comprehensive as it is spiritual (cf. Pascal's saying to the effect that man is greater than the universe). Therefore, the higher and the more comprehensive a quality, the more spiritual it is.

The word "quality" has a special meaning in dialectics. It is the property acquired by the integration of a plurality of units into one. Thus the quality (the nature) of the human body is the result of the integration of all its cells and its organs into a single organism. The same is true of personality, which is the integration into one of ideas, feelings, volitions. Now, according to this conception, if man is spiritual, the whole of Reality must be more spiritual, because man is only a part of that whole, just as a person is more spiritual than any of his parts, even his brain. Hence ultimate Reality is a Spiritual Being, who for Christians is God.

A word of caution is necessary here. The word "part" used in the above argument is inadequate, because it may lead us into the pitfall of pantheism. The cells of a body are not just parts or pieces of that body. They are organs, instruments by which the body acts in its environment of time and space. Hence the word "isolate" is preferable. An isolate is a particular aspect of the mode of existence of a universal being. In this sense the non-existence of man, indeed of the universe, would not diminish the Wholeness of Being. It would only reduce its mode of existence or manifestation in the temporal order. And although a non-manifested being is only a postulate, it is nevertheless a necessary one in order to make sense of our experience: and designates reality.

The two important principles in a line of argument of this kind are those of sacramentalism and analogy. According to the former the higher qualities are reflected, seen, exemplified in the lower qualities. According to the latter, which is the opposite of the former, we can infer the nature of the general from the particular. The integrated parts of a thing are the imperfect images of the whole, and the whole is reflected in an imperfect way in its integrated parts. Thus man is the image of God.

THE NEED FOR DYNAMIC THOUGHT

In this way the argument can be carried almost the whole way along the path of materialistic thought. There is a striking parallelism between dialectical Christianity and dialectical Materialism. It cannot of course be contended that the two are the same. But they make contact at so many points that one is driven to think that the antagonism of the two is more apparent than real, and that the causes of this antagonism are rooted in a ground other than the purely philosophical.

Space does not permit us to proceed along the whole length of this parallelism, but the excursion can profitably be made if one sets about it without prejudice. There is, however, one essential condition for this. We must abandon the old static philosophy with its impossible perplexities and insoluble contradictions, in favour of a dynamic, dialectical mode of thinking. "We have paid," said Dr. Temple recently, "too little attention to the reality of history and historical movements. We have sought some static principle of unity as the ultimate explanation of all things. But that is to desert the Bible for Hellenism." Engels in his "Ludwig Feuerbach" pleads the same cause before a different audience: "The old method of thought . . . preferred to investigate *things* as given, as fixed and stable, a method the relics of which still strongly haunt people's minds," and he advocates "a science of processes, of the origin and development of things and the interconnection which binds all the natural processes into one great whole." This frame of mind is not only necessary for our times, but it is also the background of the teaching of the Gospel. It is pre-eminently Pauline and Johannine. "Be ye perfect as your heavenly Father is perfect" is an injunction to progress. "In Him we live and move and have our being." Thus we must speak of striving towards a higher mode of life, both individually and socially. Such a mode of speech will suggest a beginning from the lowest stages of life. We must speak of an increasingly more adequate knowledge of God and of realities. This will imply a revelation ever unfolding itself. We must speak of the development of the human personality, which is the dialectical process of qualification. The conception of continual change and of movement towards perfection permeates all genuine Christian thinking. The struggle against evil, even unto death, which is *the* Christian virtue, being the virtue of the Cross, has as its purpose just that change which leads men to divine qualities. This same struggle is also the highest communist virtue, albeit in a different guise. Its purpose is the future social paradise in which all and every one will be free and happy.

BELIEFS, ACTION AND FREEDOM

An important principle in Communism is that of activism. Man must think and act at the same time. Theory must not be separated from practice, or practice from theory. This is the oneness of Faith and Works in Christianity, giving rise to Christian morality, which is man's reaction to his environment in Christ, that is society, Christ being Man as well as God. A Communist's morality is his reaction to the social environment. A Bolshevik once said to the writer:

"Man's environment must be made such that he will instinctively do the right thing. Then all the sermons will be superfluous. You Christians preach, but the environment is not changed; we set out by acting, and we change the environment,"

and he went on to say how a Russian from the dirtiest streets in Moscow, without having heard any sermons or read any "prohibitions," would not think of spitting or throwing litter about in the spotlessly clean Moscow subway. It is not an accident that in recent times activism has gathered strength in all the Christian Churches.

Another important principle which is central to Communism is man's sociality, as against a distorted conception of liberty. Morality is social and liberty, in as much as it is an isolation from society, is immoral, whether the isolation be individual or national in the form of "independence," or "autarchy," or "sovereignty." Hence unity is the requirement of morality and separatism is immoral. Therefore peace must not be sought in independence, or else independence will not be peaceful, because independence is isolation and "peace is indivisible." But isolation is the Christian sin of pride, be it individual or national. Christ is the unity of mankind and there can be no division in Christ.

The reconciliation of individual freedom and State dictatorship in the mind of a Communist is significant. For him the highest good is that freedom in which he will be able to develop his personality as he likes. For him freedom is a quality, the quality of having power over nature in all its spheres, wherever he comes into contact with it. The wider the range of his power, the freer he is. But to attain this goal and to acquire this power is utterly beyond his individual capacity. By himself and for himself he cannot create the environment necessary for such freedom. It can only be done by the social organism as a whole. In integrating himself to society, he gains this power of freedom. Hence totalitarian dictatorship. Freedom can only be bought by payment in kind. Man must forgo freedom in order to possess it. The god of freedom demands the sacrifice of freedom. This conception is Christian. Obedience to the will of God is the Christian freedom. Submission to law is a preliminary necessity in order to free oneself from its fetters. That is how the Incarnation took place. That is the process advocated and lived by apostles and saints. The alternative to this freedom is slavery to sin, that is isolation, individualism and its murderous tyranny.

THE PROSPECTS OF A NEW APOLOGETIC

In conclusion, we are justified in thinking that there is in fact a vitally important high road by which Christianity and Communism can communicate with and approach each other. In other words, there are some premises which are common to both systems. The assertions, made even by the founders of Communism themselves, that Christianity and Dialectical Materialism are mutually exclusive have not been supported by sufficiently valid arguments. It is of course obvious that an intellectual attitude of non-objection on the part of Communism to a Christian philosophy will not be satisfactory from a fully Christian point of view. In any case, the importance of apologetic, along lines of argument comprehensible to those for whom it is intended, is, especially at the present time, of paramount importance for the Church.

As to the position of the Church in a Soviet State, it can only be visualized after a thorough examination of the theoretical issues involved. Not that the ideological problems must first be settled by academic discussions—that would be stupid—but that all practical steps to clarify and to regularize the situation should be taken in conjunction with ideological steps. Every measure must be accompanied, as it were, by a preface of theoretical exposition comprehensible to the parties concerned. And, above all, the myth of the irreconcilability of Christianity and Communism must be discarded.

Can the Older Churches Learn from the Younger?

by

C. G. SCHWEITZER

Warden of the Wistow Training Centre for Post-war Christian Service

F ROM the beginning of missionary work, it has been taken for granted that the Churches which sent their missionaries to heathen lands should teach them to use the methods which in the Churches' own experience had proved the most successful.

Now the time has come to see what we in the "Christian" countries may learn from the experience of the younger Churches. We are becoming more and more aware that our so-called "Christian" countries are not as Christian as we had thought or wished. Some of them have fallen a prey to the slogans of a new pagansim or to an atheistic propaganda, and have thereby proved that their Christianity was not rooted deeply enough. Even in those countries where the test has not yet come, those with knowledge of the situation are not definitely sure what the outcome of such a test would be. Though there may be a good deal of "fossil Christianity," as Bismarck called it, the whole atmosphere cannot honestly be described as a Christian one, but as one, rather, which is mixed with indifference, agnosticism, idolatry or superstition of one sort or another.

Even the small minority of church-going people, looked at on an average, could hardly claim the name of Christian in the real sense of the early Church. How many of them would really understand St. Paul's Epistles? The worst of all is the fact that so many who have been brought up in a Christian way, who, for instance, have gone to "chapel" every morning when they were at school, are more or less immune to God's living Word; they live under the impression that they "know all about it." They stand up each Sunday and say the Creed, but have not the courage to question it, and discover and experience what it really means. There has been in Europe something like an "inflation" of religious words, even an idolization of typical terms used for centuries in the Churches. Nietzsche, one of the sharpest critics of "Christian" Europe, was right when he spoke of "the belief of so many Christians in their own belief: a sandwich is more useful than that."

It is not surprising that we face a new paganism in our time which is, on the one hand, the direct continuation of an ancient paganism never really broken, and, on the other, a definitely anti-Christian attitude on the part of people who have gone through an experience of Christianity and have deliberately discarded it. There is no doubt that the latter state of mind is much more difficult to deal with than the paganism of the natives on the mission field.

If this is the situation of the older Churches, the first step is to face the facts as they are. "The Church cannot talk to the world as though it were composed of people who were all Christians at heart" (R. A. Edwards). We must abandon all wishful thinking and pretentions, for illusionism is certainly not Christianity.

What is the significance of this, and what can we learn from the younger Churches with regard to the message itself, to the people to whom we have to take it, to the methods to be employed, to the messengers and to the response?

The message which the Churches have to bring is not an old and worn-out story, but new tidings which are always fresh, never stagnant. Otherwise it is not the right message, which comes from above and is always new and makes "anew" (*anothen*). It is not a drug which may render one immune to the next dose, but the bread which every man, woman and child needs every day afresh. People who are really hungry eat as if they did so for the first time in their lives. The only difference between the very first time and all the following is that ever since the first experience a man knows that it really satisfies his hunger.

The long history of the foreign missions has given plenty of evidence that nothing but the whole, uncompromised Gospel can meet the needs of all. We must, that is to say, do away with every tendency to blend it with civilization, or with politics, or even with morals. Is it not one of the greatest misuses of the Gospel to confuse it with a certain standard of decent and moral life, with a vague humanitarianism which thinks hopefully that with some effort man can become better and better? Jesus knew that it was the good men who were the last to accept him. Nothing else than the Gospel in all its depth and straight challenge is strong enough to bring a new spirit and new life to those who are dead though they live, or who are blind though they have eyes.

Christianity is not "another good religion," another *Weltanschauung* in addition to those which the people concerned had known before, but a new life, THE LIFE.

Nor is it merely something which happened in the past. When, forty years ago, A. Drews published his new discovery, "Jesus Never Lived," and this most modern myth was very much disputed, the Berlin City Mission held a mass meeting, the wording of the invitation to which read, not "Jesus did live," but "Jesus Christ lives."

So far as to the contents of the message, but what about the methods of bringing it home to the people? It is a great mistake to confuse the two, as some Continental theologians are inclined to do. The tendency to reject all kinds of *Anknüpfung* is, of course, a sound and necessary reaction against the reverse one of a compromising, over-psychological approach; but it is not the full truth. For *Anknüpfung* (making points of contact) must not be identified with compromising or spoiling the contents of the message. We think of St. Paul, who is a non-suspect witness, and his way of dealing with all kinds of people:

. *"I made myself servant unto all, that I might gain the more. And unto the Jews I became as a Jew, that I might gain the Jews. . . . To them that are without law, as without law, that I might gain them that are without law. . . . I am made all things to all men that I might by all means save some."*

This is not to compromise but to adapt oneself, though not the Gospel, to the special needs of one's hearers. For as the first missionary, St. Paul, and all his successors, were aware, in every nation every single individual is different from every other and needs therefore a special method of approach. To try to treat all in the same manner is not only not effective, but lacking in love. It is not enough to preach the "pure" Gospel, it must be brought home to the other side. We should be bridge-builders every time we preach: we have the task of a "pontifex," a bridge-maker, whose task is not fulfilled when he himself stands firm, but who must try to bridge the gulf between his side of the river and the other side: or, by another illustration, we should be like steel. The better the quality, the more it can be bent without breaking, the more elastic it is.

We must know as clearly as possible who and where the other man or woman is to whom we are sent to bring the ONE message, so that we may "translate" the Gospel into the language of the hearer. This is first of all, of course, a linguistic matter, but it is more than that. When Luther translated the Bible into German and gave the unsurpassed pattern to all modern translations in the world, he looked into "the mouth of the people," he listened, that is, to their way of speaking. We know what hard work our missionaries have to do until they find a term in a new dialect equivalent to a New Testament term. Do we realize into how many different "dialects" we have to translate the Bible in our own countries if our hearers are really to understand what the Bible means? This is not only a problem of words, but still more of thoughts. Are we sure that all our hearers will understand us in the same way when we speak of "sin" or of "grace," not to mention "redemption" or "justification"? In the same way as it makes all the difference whether we evangelize among primitive African tribes, or Muslims, or highly cultivated Indians, so also we must take into account whether we are dealing with peasants, or industrial workers, or, let us say, scientists. The one Biblical language will not do unless we transform its contents into the very thoughts of our hearers, which is, of course, the function of a sermon. And if we do not find the specific term in their own language we must do as the missionaries do: use their terms and transform them so that they become fit for the new idea. In other words: we must try to understand them better than they understand themselves, for Christianity not only answers the questions they ask, but deepens them and even raises new ones of which they had not been aware.

Take, for instance, a doctor. If he is honest he can be brought to recognize the limitations of his work and the truth of the old saying: *Medicus curat, natura sanat.* He can realize that with all his scientific skill he cannot really heal anyone; he can only remove the obstacles. The problem of life, which is behind all work of healing, is not mainly a material one, a matter of drugs and splints, but on a deeper level a psychological—nay, more, a spiritual—one, because it is a total, and therefore a personal, one.

Or take the general attitude of scientists which leaves room for no level of truth beside their own. The older Churches, in order to make their message acceptable, have tended to adapt themselves and their message to the scientific outlook. Of course they must respect science in its own sphere, and not try to interfere with its results in an amateur way; but they have so often failed to question the spiritual and metaphysical presuppositions of scientists when they consciously or unconsciously overstep the limits of their true scientific sphere. The Churches therefore became "apologetical"—that is, on the defensive—in their own sphere, instead of being aware of St. Paul's words: "We are more than conquerors." They began to apologize for their very existence in a world that did not accept them, instead of challenging that world.

An agnostic once said: "Before central Africa was explored, people could have what opinions they liked about it. They could, for instance, believe that the heat in the desert is due to a great furnace there. But now that it has been explored, there is no room for believing such nonsense, for we know what is there. If there was a time for belief, it is now past, because science has replaced it by knowledge."

Do not many Christians adapt themselves to this attitude—for instance, when they say: "Can we still believe in miracles?" This little word "still" is, in fact, a worm in the tree of the Churches. It presupposes, or does not reject the presupposition, that there will be a time when Christianity will definitely be out of date, when modern man will need it no longer, when scientific truth will have taken over the space formerly held by Christian truth and faith.

We must and can show the scientists that their truths, even in their own minds, cannot be the final truths, but that behind and underneath and above these particular truths stands the Truth, comprehending all truths. The old world has reached, or at least is reaching, the stage at which it becomes only too clear that all scientific and technical work, separated from its centre in God, is a complete failure and must by necessity lead to chaos. To accept the one central and personal Truth does not mean losing any precious values, but, on the contrary, regaining them at a new and higher level, in a fuller and more universal sense.

This does not imply, of course, that we should attempt the impossible, as was done in vain in former times: to prove the Gospel in a logical way. No, the truth of the Gospel will make itself evident if we remove obstacles which prevent people from understanding its real meaning. For the Gospel, or, better still, Jesus Christ Himself, is the supreme answer to all human questions and problems. We, as "pontifices," as bridge-makers, have only to lead up to the way, to show how individual problems, either conscious or unconscious, are answered by the one Truth.

And another point: let us not underrate the power of collective thought. We have to face the same amount of "caste" prejudices in the lands to which we are native as the missionaries encounter among the natives of other lands. It is all the same whether the creed is called Capitalism, Socialism, Fascism or Atheism. Even those who call all religions "opiate for the people" may be possessed by one of these opiates without knowing it, and cling to it with enthusiasm.

If we encounter such an enthusiasm, as we do, for instance, in the Nazi, we cannot overcome it by belittling his cause, but by offering him a cause which is still more worthy of the same or of a purer enthusiasm. In order to arrest a fire in a forest you must light a counter-fire.

But who spreads the Gospel? In the younger Churches we

speak of "missionaries"—that is, men and women "sent out," sent out into the pagan world. They must be prepared to be witnesses—that is, according to the original meaning of the word, martyrs; yet martyrs not only in the body, but also in dying again and again in their daily life, being ready to give up all privileges and personal comfort. Are those who preach the gospel in the older Churches prepared to do the same and to pay the cost? As it is, we cannot wonder that so few are touched by the message, for they do not see any difference in the lives of those who profess to be Christian, and they see that the corporate life of these so-called Christians is in no way distinguished from that of the non-Christians. The "social Gospel" is not to be preached, but lived. If those who are privileged to proclaim the Gospel are bridge-builders, are they prepared also to be used as bridges on which our fellow men may tread? It is true that we cannot prevent them from being challenged by the stumbling-block of Christ's Cross, but let us not make the mistake of confusing this One stumbling-block, which cannot be avoided, with the stumbling-blocks which we actually become in our own very imperfect persons.

Finally, what of the response to our message? Would the missionaries be satisfied if the number of true Christians were never to increase? In our Churches we have very clearly lost the expectation that something may happen when we have brought home our message to our listeners, that the most "natural" result of the preaching of the Gospel is that new people will be won. And these new Christians will only prove to be true followers of Christ when they proclaim the Gospel themselves. Believing and professing the Gospel should mean one and the same thing. What would it mean for the spreading of Christianity if all who become Christians become living witnesses and are "ready to give an answer to every man that asketh a reason of the hope that is in them" (1 Pet. iii. 15). "Christians are the Bible which the world reads." Without them even the best work of our Bible societies is in vain. The officiating priests cannot do the work alone; every single Christian must regard himself as a missionary, able and willing to "translate" the Gospel to his fellows in all stations of life.

In this way our Churches would become real communities, as the young Churches have once more taught us. A genuine "building up of a community out of the Gospel," as Gutmann has described it when speaking of his work among African tribes on the slopes of Kilimanjaro; that is the task we have to do here at home as well. That means that our often stagnant parishes would become once more creative, finding new expressions for the old and ever fresh story, as Gutmann, Keysser and others have experienced; building up in the midst of a decaying world fertile oases from which new life can flow into the desert.

Either the Churches will become evangelizing Churches, or they will fade away. They must evangelize, however, not only among the heathen, but among their own people as well, and we shall have to learn from the immense work which is going on in the mission fields. For, as a German novelist, himself the son of a missionary, put it in one of his novels, where an Indian Brahmin speaks of true Christianity: "I am certain that Christian history has scarcely yet begun."